Favorite Sons of Civil War Kentucky

Bryan S. Bush

The History Press

Published by The History Press
Charleston, SC
www.historypress.net

Back cover image of Mill Springs, Kentucky battlefield taken by author. Front cover image courtesy of the Library of Congress.

First published 2017

Manufactured in the United States

ISBN 9781625859938

Library of Congress Control Number: 2017948453

Notice: The information in this book is true and complete to the best of our knowledge. It is offered without guarantee on the part of the author or The History Press. The author and The History Press disclaim all liability in connection with the use of this book.

Contents

Acknowledgements

I would like to thank the Old Bardstown Village Inc. and, in particular, Steve Munson for allowing me to photograph the amazing collection of artifacts at the Civil War Battles of the Western Theater Museum. This site, in Bardstown, Kentucky, features the "War of the West." The Civil War Museum was opened in 1988 in the old waterworks building in Bardstown, and between 1988 and 1992, it served more than 250,000 visitors. Between 1992 and 1996, the museum was totally renovated and was incorporated into the Kentucky State Parks system. It officially reopened on June 29, 1996, to the pleasure of Civil War buffs from around the world. The Civil War Museum also has an 1800s pioneer village adjacent to the site featuring several original log cabins in order to depict life during these times. The museum complex also features education on women's role during the Civil War museum and a war memorial museum, which is dedicated to all the wars in which the United States has fought, from the American Revolution to Desert Storm.

I would like to thank the Louisville Free Public Library for allowing me access to its research tools and, in particular, Joseph Hardesty.

I would like to thank Cave Hill Cemetery in Louisville, Kentucky, for its support throughout the years and, in particular, Michael Higgs, coordinator of the Cave Hill Heritage Foundation. Cave Hill Cemetery is Louisville's premier cemetery. The purpose of the Cave Hill Heritage Foundation is to secure funding for the long-term preservation of this unique cemetery. Specifically, the mission of the Cave Hill Heritage Foundation is threefold:

TO RESTORE THE HISTORICAL MONUMENTS AND BUILDINGS.
Cave Hill Cemetery is known for its exquisite collection of monumental art, many examples of which are more than 150 years old. Additionally, the property includes a variety of historic structures, from the administration office to the board room to the three-and-a-half-mile wall of brick and stone that encircles the perimeter. The resources provided through the foundation will allow cemetery management to be proactive both in addressing specific, long-term conservation projects and in responding to critical situations that require immediate intervention and stabilization.

TO PRESERVE THE ARBORETUM SETTING.
On average, fifty trees are removed each year at Cave Hill Cemetery due to disease, old age or weather damage, and more than one hundred plants are replaced. The Cave Hill Heritage Foundation will help provide resources for the unexpected, as well as help preserve and sustain the beauty of the cemetery's arboretum setting. It will provide for the removal and the replacement of specimen trees and shrubs to ensure that future generations will have access to this amazing green space in the heart of Louisville.

TO PROVIDE COMMUNITY EDUCATION AND AWARENESS.
The history of Cave Hill Cemetery is inextricably tied to the history of Louisville. Through its landscape and monuments, the cemetery tells the story of this beloved city by the river and its remarkable citizenry. The Cave Hill Heritage Foundation will help provide resources to produce educational materials, expand public awareness and develop special events and programs for schoolchildren and the community at large. It will also ensure that the critical task of recording and archiving the history of the cemetery will continue.

I would also like to thank my parents, Carol and Gene Bush, and stepmom, JoAnn Bush, for their support. I would also like to thank my friend Ryan Reynolds for support and inspiration.

Introduction

In the 1860 election, Kentucky was divided as to who to vote for president. Many Kentucky residents voted for John Bell of Tennessee, who stood for adherence to the Union and maintaining slavery. Other Kentucky residents voted for native son John C. Breckinridge, who was for the Southern Democratic Party, which supported slavery and secession. Some Kentucky residents voted for Stephen Douglas, who was on the Democratic ticket. Very few Kentucky residents voted for native son Abraham Lincoln, who ran on the Republican ticket that stood for the elimination of slavery. Kentucky was a slaveholding state. Kentucky wanted to maintain the institution of slavery and remain loyal to the Union.

When the Civil War began on April 12, 1861, when shots were fired on Fort Sumter, South Carolina, Kentucky had to decide whether to stay in the Union or join the Confederacy. In May, the state voted for neutrality. Although Kentucky may have remained neutral, thousands of Kentucky's brave sons decided that they could not sit the war out and decided to join the Union or the Confederacy. Recruitment agents for the two opposing sides lined the streets of Louisville, Kentucky, asking for volunteers. Union recruits were sent to Camp Joseph Holt in Indiana or Camp Dick Robinson in Garrard County, Kentucky. Those who were recruited for the Confederacy left for New Orleans or Camp Boone in Tennessee. More than 100,000 sons of Kentucky served in the Union army in the Civil War. Between 25,000 and 40,000 Kentucky soldiers fought for the Confederacy.

Kentucky soldiers served in both the Eastern Theater and Western Theater of the Civil War. They fought in battles such as Bull Run, Gettysburg, Antietam and Appomattox. They also fought in the battles for Fort Henry and Fort Donelson, as well as at Shiloh, Baton Rouge, Stone's River, Vicksburg, Chickamauga, Atlanta and in South Carolina.

Kentucky soldiers served under Confederate generals such as native Kentuckians John Hunt Morgan, John C. Breckinridge and others such as John Bell Hood, William Hardee, Nathan Bedford Forrest and Thomas "Stonewall" Jackson. Union Kentucky soldiers fought under men like William T. Sherman and Ulysses S. Grant.

The purpose of this book is to cover Kentucky soldiers who fought for the Union or Confederacy and who made major impacts on Kentucky's history during and after the Civil War. Such examples are Confederate Colonel Philip Lee, who fought in the 1st Kentucky Brigade, also known as the Orphan Brigade. After the Civil War, he became one of the leading prosecuting attorneys in Louisville. For the Union side, Colonels William Boone and J. Rowan Boone served in the 28th Kentucky Union Infantry. Both would become prominent attorneys in Kentucky. William Boone would become related to the Rowan family through marriage and became the attorney for Rebecca Rowan, who was widowed when John Rowan Jr. died through an accident at his home Federal Hill in Bardstown. Rebecca Rowan was burdened with financial debt from her husband, and William Boone helped her until his death. Federal Hill later became known as My Old Kentucky Home. Another example would be David Yandell, who was the chief medical director for Confederate General Albert Sidney Johnston. After the Civil War, he became a prominent doctor and taught medicine at the University of Louisville. After his death, an auditorium was named after him in honor of his medical efforts.

The book also includes soldiers who settled in Kentucky after the Civil War and made major contributions to the community. Perry Wilkes, who was awarded the Congressional Medal of Honor as a civilian when he was a U.S. pilot during the Civil War, led a successful life after the war, commanding a fleet of steamboats. Another example is Sergeant Major Joel Womack, who helped found the Jockey Club and the Kentucky Derby.

The book also includes civilians who made major contributions to the Civil War. Norvin Green was a pioneer in the telegraph industry. He started a telegraph line running from New Orleans to Louisville, Kentucky, during the war. After the war, he bought several telegraph companies and formed them into one huge telegraph company, known as the Western

Union Telegraph Company. Washington Wyatt was a local undertaker in Louisville who, during the Civil War, buried thousands of Union and Confederate soldiers. After the war, he continued to serve as Louisville's preeminent undertaker. William Shakespeare Hays claimed that he was the author of "Dixie" and wrote more than two hundred songs during his career. He was also a poet and steamboat pilot.

Chapter 1

Perry Wilkes

Perry Wilkes was born in Southern Indiana on June 6, 1830. In 1844, he started his river life as a flatboat pilot. He lived in New Albany, Indiana, for a number of years and later moved to Leavenworth, Indiana. On November 11, 1861, he enrolled in the 49th Indiana Infantry, Company F, in Jeffersonville, Indiana. The 49th was organized in Jeffersonville and was mustered into service on November 11, 1861. The regiment fought skirmishes at Big Tree Gap and Cumberland Gap. On February 8, 1862, Wilkes was promoted to a second lieutenant. In June 1862, the regiment accompanied General George Morgan's forces to the Cumberland Gap, and that November, the regiment joined Union General William T. Sherman's expedition to Vicksburg, Mississippi. At the Battle of Chickasaw Bluffs, the regiment suffered fifty-six casualties in wounded and killed and was in the expedition against Arkansas Post. The men assisted in digging a canal across Young's Point and moved to the rear of Vicksburg. The regiment participated in the battles of Port Gibson, Champion's Hill and Black River. On March 22, 1863, at Milliken's Bend, Louisiana, Wilkes resigned from the 49th Indiana Infantry and joined the United States Navy as a civilian pilot. Wilkes was assigned to the tinclad gunboat USS *Signal*.

In March 1864, President Abraham Lincoln authorized an expedition against Shreveport, Louisiana. Shreveport was the headquarters of Confederate General Edmund Kirby Smith and a major supply depot and gateway to Texas. The plan called for a large combined naval and infantry force under Admiral David Porter and Major General Nathaniel

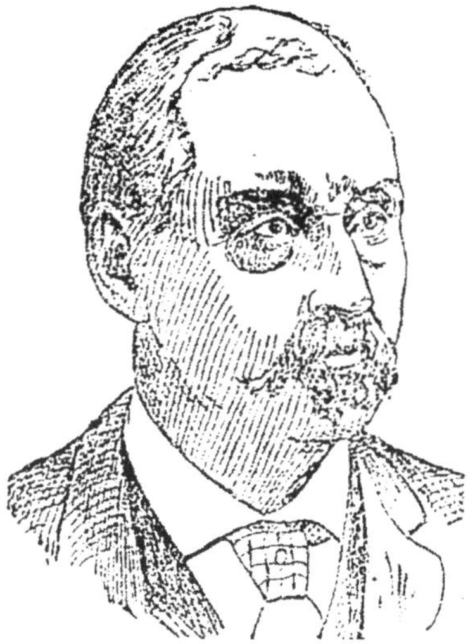

Captain Perry Wilkes. *Courtesy of the* Louisville Courier Journal, *March 21, 1889.*

Banks to move up the Red River to Shreveport. Porter's gunboats would provide artillery support and serve as troop transports for a ten-thousand-man contingent sent by Major General William T. Sherman and commanded by Brigadier General Andrew Smith. An additional fifteen thousand men under Major General Frederick Steele coming from Little Rock, Arkansas, were to join the main force before the attack on Shreveport.

Also in March, Union forces under Porter and Smith captured Fort De Russy, which the Confederates depended on to protect the river. On March 19, Federals occupied Alexandria, Louisiana. There, General Ulysses S. Grant ordered Banks to return to New Orleans. Grant also ordered Smith to return his command to Sherman. Delays put the Federals behind schedule. The campaign began to fall apart. On April 8, Banks was defeated at Mansfield, forty miles south of Shreveport. The following day, on April 9, the retreating Federal army made a stand at Pleasant Hill and won, but Banks continued to retreat. Any further movement against Shreveport was out of the question, and Smith's forces rejoined Porter. The gunboats retraced their course down the Red River.[1]

On May 4, 1864, Union Lieutenant Edward Morgan, who commanded the USS *Signal*, received orders from Rear Admiral David Dixon Porter to take on the bearer of dispatches from Union General Nathaniel Banks and proceed downriver until he overtook the USS *Covington*, under the command of Lieutenant George Lord, which was protecting the army transport steamer *John Warner*. Morgan was to accompany the *Covington* and *Warner* until they linked up with the flagship *Black Hawk*, which was anchored at the mouth of the Black River, and then return to Fort De Russy, await the arrival of a gunboat and then proceed upriver to Alexandria.

At 11:00 a.m., with Wilkes at the wheel, the USS *Signal* got underway and proceeded down the river. About ten miles below Alexandria, Morgan met a party of men from the 120th Ohio Infantry who reported their escape from the transport *City Belle*. The *City Belle* had been captured and destroyed that

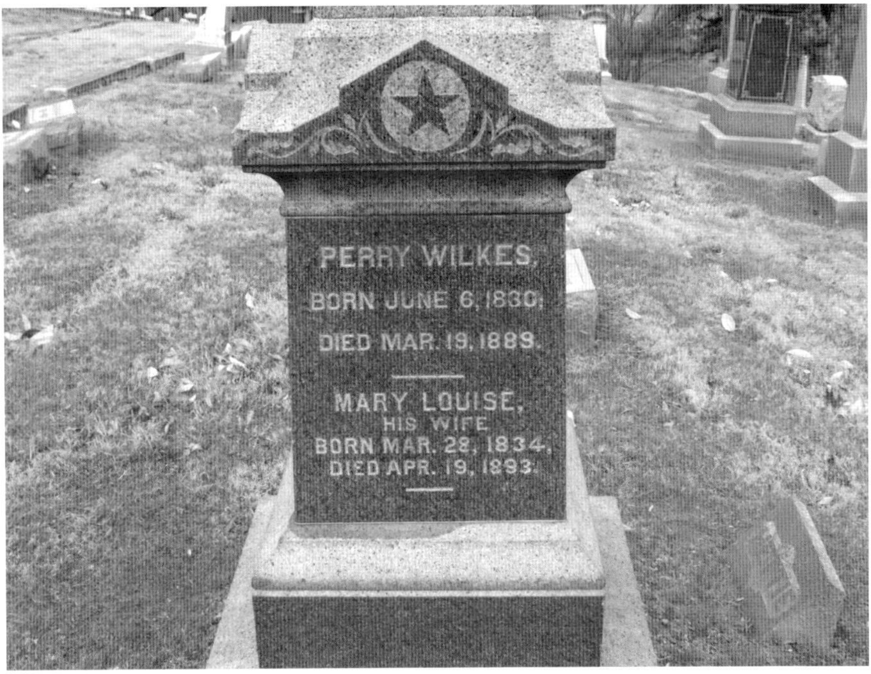

Above: Close-up of the Captain Perry Wilkes Monument, Cave Hill Cemetery. *Photograph taken by the author.*

Right: Perry Wilkes Monument, Cave Hill Cemetery. *Photograph taken by the author.*

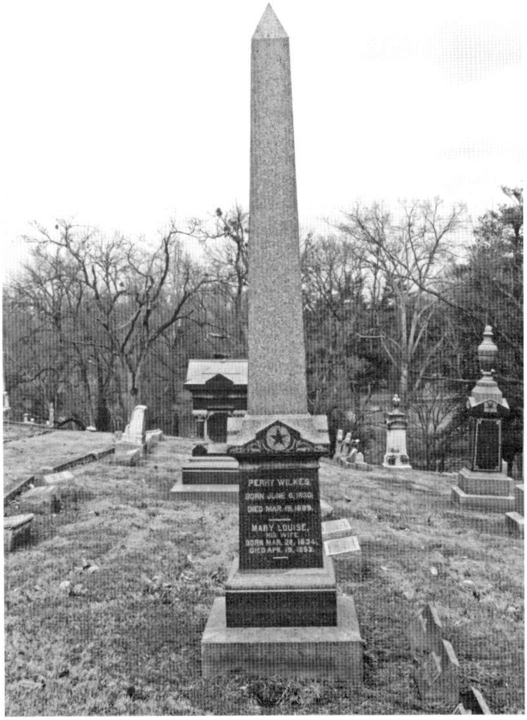

morning by Confederate artillery and infantry located about fifteen or twenty miles down the river from their location. About ten miles down the river at Wilson's plantation, the *Signal* was fired upon by a party of Confederate cavalry. Morgan returned fire from the starboard guns and passed by the Confederate cavalry. As soon as they rounded the next bend, the *Signal* was fired upon by a party of Rebel cavalry.

About four miles below Wilson's plantation, Morgan came upon the USS *Covington* and *Warner*. The men of the *Covington* were repairing its rudder. Both the *Signal* and *Covington* kept up an irregular fire during the night on the right-hand shore, since the Confederate infantry continued to fire on both ships, while the *Covington* was trying to repair the damage. At 4:30 a.m., all three ships—the USS *Signal*, USS *Covington* and *John Warner*—got underway, with the *Warner* in the lead, the *Covington* next and the *Signal* last.[2]

At Dunn's Bayou, they were fired upon by two pieces of Confederate artillery and infantry. The *Covington* was hit by the Confederate battery only three times and the *Warner*'s rudders were disabled, but the *Warner* continued downstream until it came to a short point in the river, where the ship went into the bank. The *Warner* had no sooner struck the bank when a Rebel battery on the right shore going down, along with between four and five thousand Confederate infantry, opened fire upon the *Warner* and the *Covington*. The

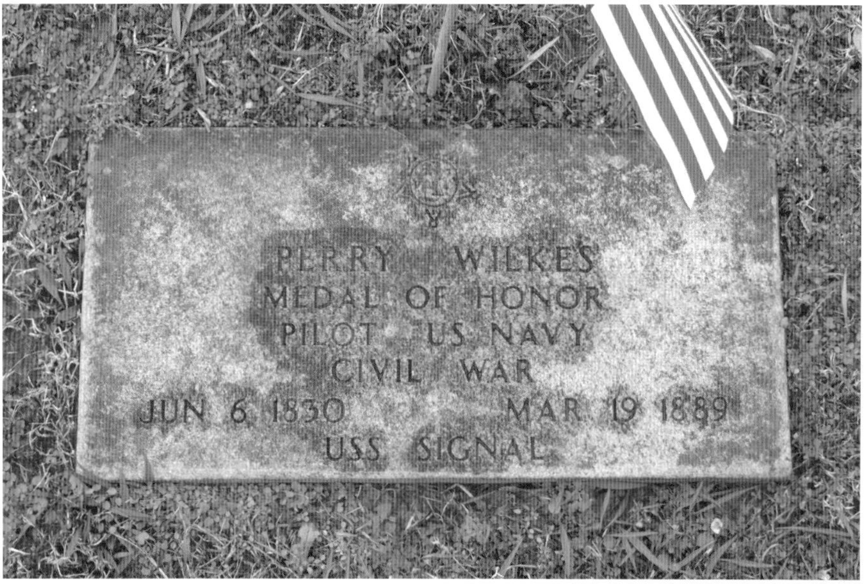

Close-up of Perry Wilkes's tombstone. *Photograph taken by the author.*

Covington and *Signal* immediately opened fire. Almost every Confederate shot hit boilers, steam pipes or machinery on the *Warner*, as the vessel was only one hundred yards away from the Confederate batteries. After Lord and Morgan engaged the Confederates for three hours, the *Warner* hoisted the white flag. The *Covington* and *Signal* continued to fire.

Lieutenant Lord sent a party, which left the ship under severe fire to burn the *Warner*, but the Union colonel aboard the *Warner* sent word that 125 men had been killed and wounded and requested that the ship not be burned. The request was granted. A short time later, Wilkes sent word to Lieutenant Lord that his ship, the USS *Signal*, had been disabled. The wheel had literally been shot out of Wilkes's hands by a bursting shell. Lieutenant Lord came alongside the *Signal* and took the ship into tow, starting upstream. Lord ordered Wilkes to go into the pilothouse of the *Covington* and assist with the pilots. Wilkes found Frank McCloskey and Mr. Emerson piloting the ship. Mr. Emerson asked if Wilkes would remain and assist McCloskey while he checked on the rudders. Wilkes had been in the pilothouse for about twenty minutes when word came that the *Covington*'s rudders had been disabled and the *Signal* had begun to drift. A Union officer yelled up to the pilothouse to Wilkes and McCloskey that the ship would be abandoned.[3] Lieutenant Lord realized that he could not pass the *Warner*. Knowing that the *Signal* would drift toward the *Warner* and the Rebels would immediately board the ship, Lord ordered the commanding officer to anchor the ship.

Lieutenant Lord took his ship upstream on the opposite shore. He used his stern guns to fire on the lower battery, his broadside on the infantry abreast of him and his bow guns on battery that was ahead of them, which had been brought down from Dunn's Bayou. Lord tied his ship to the bank for an hour. A shell struck his boilers, letting out all the steam. Lord's ammunition was exhausted, and his howitzers were disabled by the cracked bolts drawing out and every shot coming through the ship. Lord decided to burn the ship and spike the guns. Lord and his men, along with Wilkes, were captured.[4]

As for the *Signal*, the ship drifted toward the shore. Morgan hoped that he could set his ship ablaze and escape with his crew, but his ship drifted higher up the shore than he expected. Nearing the shore, Morgan called for volunteers to get a line out. A line from the ship was secured to the shore. While men from the ship began to secure the ship to the shore and secure a route for escape up an embankment, the Confederates began to fire volleys into the ship. Morgan tried to drop the ship astern but got stuck in the mud. Immediately upon reaching the shore, Morgan gave permission for all who chose to do so to escape up the bank and ordered for preparations for the ship to be burned. Before Morgan was able to set his ship ablaze, the Confederate forces decided to concentrate their efforts to prevent the *Signal* crew from escaping, as the *Warner* and *Covington* were already out of commission. A battery above and below the *Signal* directed its shells on the only possible route of escape, while 1,500 sharpshooters poured volleys of Minié balls into the path of the hurricane deck. Morgan had no choice but to surrender. Morgan reported that the casemate of the deck was penetrated eleven or twelve times by shot and shell and that two shells went through the pilothouse and carried away part of the wheel. The *Signal* had been hit thirty-eight times in four minutes. Morgan lost 25 killed and 13 wounded.[5]

Eventually, Wilkes was exchanged, and on April 11, 1865, Secretary of the Navy Gideon Wells awarded Wilkes the Naval Congressional Medal of honor under General Order No. 5, to date from December 31, 1864, for his "gallant and meritorious conduct while serving as pilot of the USS *Signal* in the Red River." The Medal of Honor was the first awarded in the Civil War. On November 21, 1861, President Abraham Lincoln signed a bill containing the provision for the medal for the navy to be given to petty officers, seaman, landsmen and Marines who distinguished themselves by their gallantry and other seamanlike qualities. On July 12, 1862, legislation was passed to include the army for the Medal of Honor. During the Civil War, the Medal of Honor was the highest military decoration attainable by a member of the United States armed forces. Of the 3,464 medals awarded to date, 1,522 were awarded during the Civil War, including the one for Perry Wilkes.

After the Civil War, in 1870, Wilkes moved to Louisville and was engaged for fourteen years with the Louisville and Evansville mail line as captain and pilot. He was commander of the *Palestine* and pilot on the *Tarascon*, *Morning Star*, *Gray Eagle* and *James Guthrie*. After leaving the company, he spent four years as a towboat pilot between Pittsburgh and New Orleans for J.C. Risher & Company and Joseph Walton & Company. Wilkes was known as one of the best steamboat men between Pittsburg and New Orleans. He married Mary Louise Romine and had eleven children. He died on March 19, 1899, and is buried at Cave Hill Cemetery.[6]

Chapter 2

Union Colonels William Boone and J. Rowan Boone

Colonel William P. Boone was born on October 12, 1813, in Boone Township, Harrison County, Indiana. His father was Colonel Samuel Boone. William Boone's grandfather was a first cousin to Daniel Boone. William Boone was educated at Corydon, Indiana, which was at the time Indiana's state capital. When he turned seventeen, he studied law under Judge William A. Porter, who was the leading lawyer in Indiana. On October 16, 1836, William was licensed to practice law and became a partner with Judge Porter.[7]

William Boone gained the attention of the Honorable W.P. Thomasson of Louisville. Thomasson asked Boone to enter into a partnership with him in Louisville. Boone moved to Louisville and began a practice in the firm of Thomasson and Boone. Thomasson returned to Congress, the firm dissolved and the firm of Boone and Clark continued the business. Boone and his relative Charles Pennebaker formed a partnership as Boone and Pennebaker. He married Miss Eliza Harney, the only child of Dr. John Milton Harney, whose wife was a daughter of Judge John Rowan, who was a distinguished layer and statesman and raised his granddaughter, Mrs. Boone, both her parents having died when she was an infant. Judge John Rowan owned Federal Hill in Bardstown, Kentucky, which later became My Old Kentucky Home state park. William Boone and Eliza Harney had John Rowan Boone, Samuel Boone and Annie Boone. The ties between the Rowans and Boones remained close.[8] When John Rowan Jr. died from falling out the second-story window at Federal Hill on August 14, 1855, his

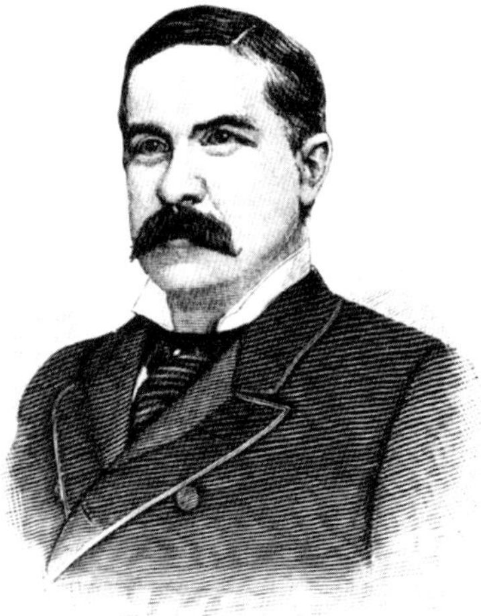

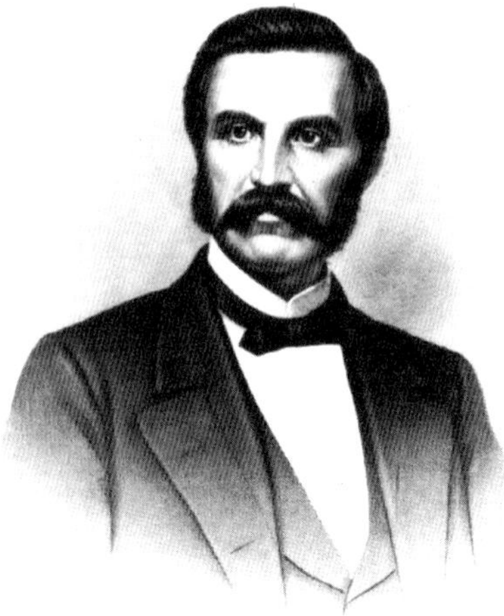

Left: Colonel John Rowan Boone. *From E. Polk Johnson's* History of the Ohio Falls Cities and Their Counties: General History with Illustrations and Biographical Sketches, *vol. 1 (1882).*

Right: Colonel William Boone. *From E. Polk Johnson's* History of the Ohio Falls Cities and Their Counties: General History with Illustrations and Biographical Sketches, *vol. 1 (1882).*

wife, Rebecca, had the burden of raising ten children and was left with the management of a farm, some slaves and the unsettled estate of her father-in-law. Rebecca Rowan's chief counsel was William Boone. Boone served as Rebecca's legal advisor and confidant until his death in 1875.[9]

John Rowan Boone, William's son, attended Louisville schools and spent most of his time in horsemanship and hunting. In 1861, John was a student of the Indiana University in Bloomington, Indiana.[10]

In early 1861, William Boone and Pennebaker were elected as Union candidates to the Kentucky legislature. William Boone also recruited Home Guards for the defense of Louisville. Some of these companies went into Camp Joe Holt across the river in Indiana, while others remained in Louisville and did not go into the U.S. service until the days of neutrality were passed. Colonel Boone commanded the companies belonging to the west end of Louisville, and Colonel Curran Pope commanded those in the east end of the city. In June 1861, John Boone quit Indiana University, joined the "Boone Guards" and became a lieutenant in the company. When the Confederates invaded Kentucky and captured Bowling Green in September 1861, Union General Lovell Rousseau led the companies from Louisville to Muldraugh's Hill, where they remained several days, and then returned to Louisville.[11]

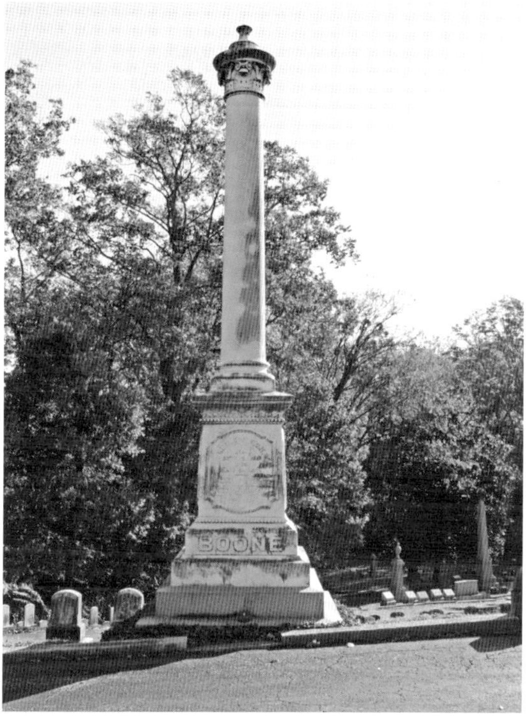

Left: Boone family monument, Cave Hill Cemetery. *Photograph taken by the author.*

Below: William Boone engraving on family monument. *Photograph taken by the author.*

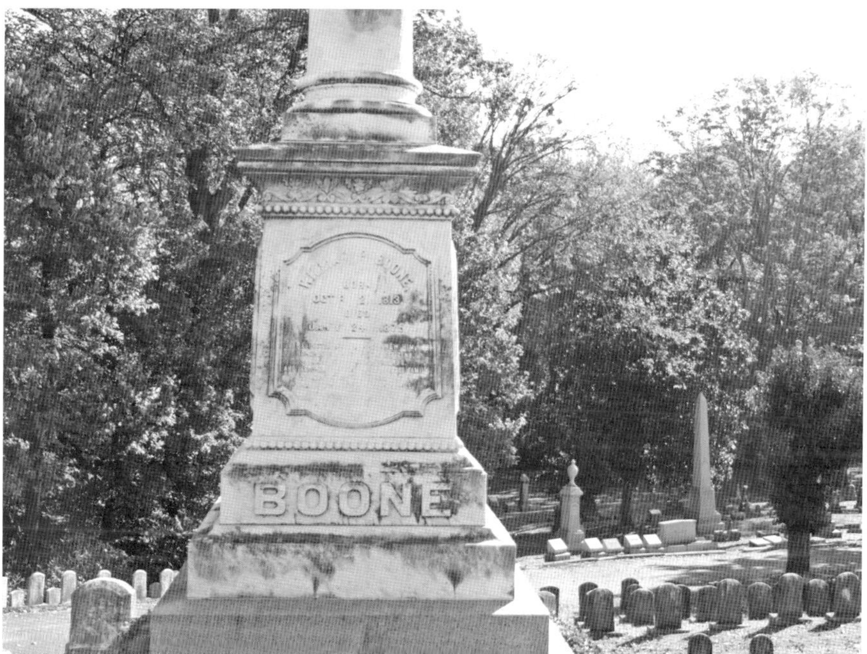

Upon return of the Home Guards to Louisville, Colonel Boone was authorized to raise a regiment for the United States. Nearly the whole six or seven Home Guard companies enlisted under Colonel Boone and other men of Louisville joined with them, and the 28th Kentucky Infantry was born. John Rowan Boone, son of the colonel, also joined the 28th Kentucky.[12]

Around October 1, the 28th Kentucky obtained tents and went into camp at Shepherdsville. In December, it moved to New Haven. In 1862, the 28th Kentucky protected the Louisville and Nashville Railroad. In June, four companies were on the Lebanon Branch, and other companies were at Bowling Green and Franklin, Kentucky. The regiment was assigned to Union General Ebenezer Dumont's brigade, Union General Don Carlos Buell's army. In July, two companies with Colonel Boone were at Gallatin, Tennessee, and were scattered all along the railroad, with 120 men. Confederate General John Hunt Morgan captured Colonel Boone and burned the railroad at Gallatin. Colonel Boone was exchanged, and after an investigation, Colonel Boone was absolved from any blame and rejoined his command at Clarksville, Tennessee.[13]

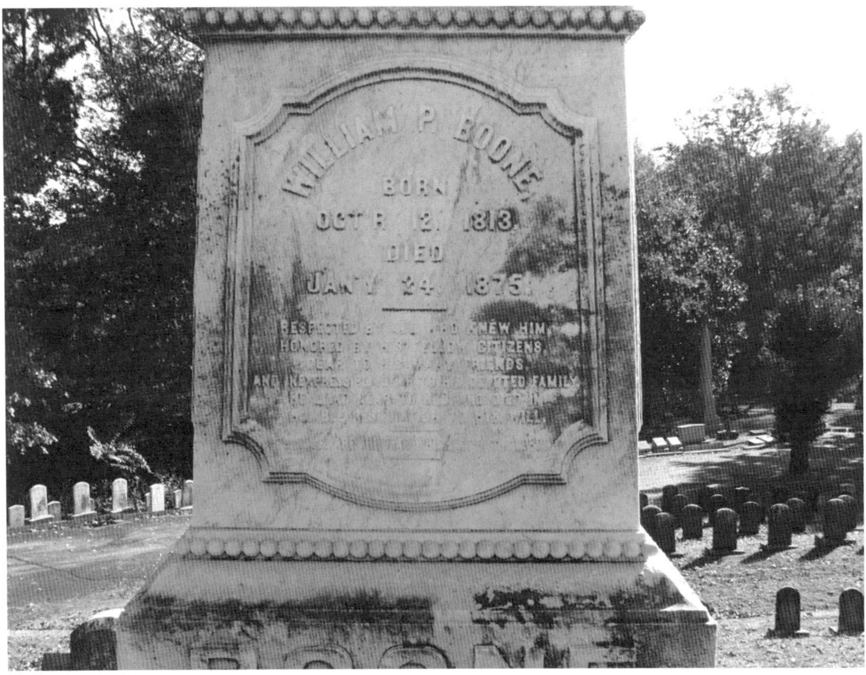

Close-up of William Boone's engraving on family monument. *Photograph taken by the author.*

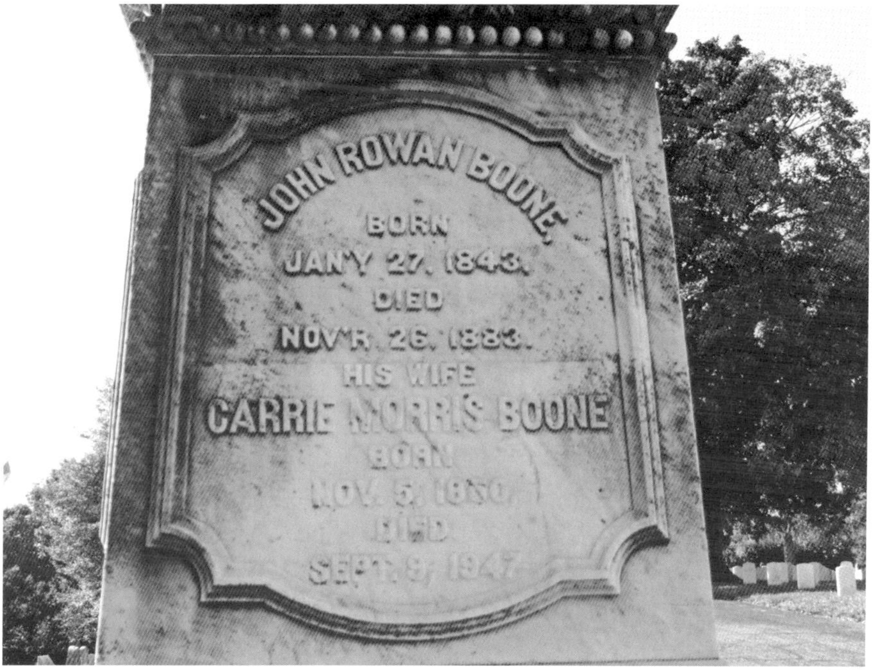

Close-up of John Rowan Boone's engraving on family monument. *Photograph taken by the author.*

While at Clarksville and Columbia, Tennessee, the 28th Kentucky Infantry became mounted by orders of General Rosecrans. The 28th Kentucky did continuous duty around the state of Tennessee and engaged the Confederates in many small skirmishes. The regiment served with Union General William Rosecrans's army in all of its operations up to and including the Battle of Chickamauga in September 1863. During the battle, the 28th Kentucky did scouting and outpost duty, being on the flanks of the Union army and associated with the cavalry. On December 23, 1863, Union General George Thomas, General W.C. Whittaker and Governor Thomas Bramlette of Kentucky obtained a commission of lieutenant colonel for John Boone. Colonel William Boone became commander of a brigade comprising the 3rd and 5th Kentucky Cavalry, 4th Michigan Cavalry and the 28th Kentucky Mounted Infantry. The men of the 28th Kentucky were mounted and armed with Spencer repeating rifles.[14]

In January 1864, the 28th Kentucky became a Veteran Infantry regiment, which meant that the regiment reenlisted for three more years. The regiment was kept on continuous duty around Chattanooga. On January 21, Colonel

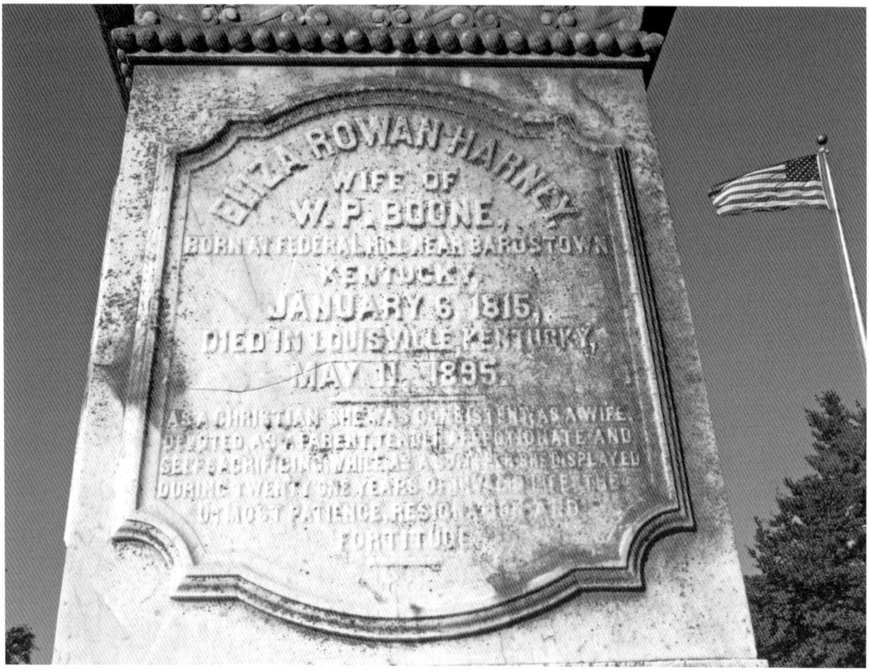

Close-up of Eliza Rowan Harney's engraving on family monument. Notice the monument states that she was born at Federal Hill near Bardstown, Kentucky. *Photograph taken by the author.*

Boone moved out of camp at Rossville, Georgia, at 10:00 a.m., with the 28th Kentucky Mounted Infantry, the 4th Michigan Cavalry, under Captain Alfred Abell, consisting of a force of 431 men and 15 officers. The command moved in the direction of and through McLemore's Cove to a point between Blue Nird Gap and Dug Gap, twenty-five miles south of Chattanooga, and camped for the night, placing strong pickets on the approaches through those gaps.[15]

At 3:00 a.m., the march resumed. Crossing Lookout at the intersection of Pigeon Mountain, the group passed through Broomtown Valley to Summersville, then across Taylor's Ridge to Dirt Town and then eight miles in the direction of Dalton to the camp of Colonel Culberson, commanding the Home Guards, where three hundred men were routed. The camp was destroyed, but the main body of the Confederates escaped in the direction of Dalton, where the Confederates were strongly posted.[16]

Colonel Boone moved back in the direction of Chattanooga, re-crossed Taylor's Ridge and camped for the night three miles from Summerville.

The command had marched fifty-nine miles and captured one government wagon and fifteen prisoners, including a Confederate Captain Hubbard. At 5:00 a.m., Colonel Boone moved toward Rossville and arrived in camp at 10:00 p.m.[17]

In February 1864, Colonel W.P. Boone, remaining under General George Thomas, south of Chattanooga, picketed the roads in the direction of Lafayette, Resaca and Dalton. In March, the regiment was sent to Pulaski, Tennessee, where it was associated with the 2nd Kentucky Cavalry. In April, the regiment returned to the vicinity of Chattanooga and was stationed at Lee and Gordon's Mills. On April 18, the regiment was transferred by order of General George Thomas from the 14th Corps to the 4th Corps and assigned to George D.Wagner's brigade, 2nd Division. At that time, the regiment was dismounted.[18]

On May 2, 1864, Wagner's brigade—which consisted of the 40th and 57th Indiana, the 26th and 97th Ohio, the 28th Kentucky and the 100th Illinois Infantry, with the rest of General John Newton's division—marched from Cleveland south on the road leading toward Dalton, Georgia. All arrived at Catoosa Springs on May 5. On May 7, the brigade moved out, heading toward Tunnel Hill. It arrived at the tannery and camped one and a half miles from the town. On May 8, the brigade moved east into the valley that surrounded the northern extremity of Rocky Face Ridge, for the purpose of supporting General Charles Harker's brigade, which had driven the Confederates from their advanced position and effected a lodgement on the ridge. Once they arrived, no Confederates could be seen, and they returned to camp at the tannery.

On May 9, General Newton ordered the brigade on the crest of Rocky Face, on the left of General Harker's brigade. The nature of the ground threw Wagner's brigade into line on the ridge at right angles with the Confederates' works, which were on the east side of the ridge and in plain view from their position. In the afternoon, General Newton directed Wagner to swing his left forward, for the purpose of joining the right of General John Schofield's Corps, which was moving in line down the valley on the east side of Rocky Face, with the view of surrounding the Confederate works. Wagner, however, was unable to join General Schofield's right flank without losing his connection with the left of Harker's brigade, which Wagner was directing to maintain and support in event of his making an attack. Adjusting his lines with Harker's left, Wagner moved cautiously upon the Confederates works until the skirmishers on his right regiment became engaged, the Confederates opening furiously with their muskets.

At about this time, a portion of Harker's brigade assaulted the Confederates on the crest of the ridge but was unable to carry the works, and Wagner withdrew his command and took position on the top of the ridge. After dark, Wagner relieved General Harker's brigade with his, and having taken measures to avoid surprise, his brigade camped for the night. With the exception of picket firing, the lines remained quiet during that night and the next day.[19]

On the evening of May 10, Wagner's brigade was relieved by the 1st Brigade, under Colonel Sherman, and Wagner withdrew farther north along the ridge. On May 11, Wagner was ordered to take a position on the north end of Rocky Face, where he remained overnight. On the morning of May 12, at daylight, Wagner was directed to march his brigade into the valley on the west side of the ridge and took position in the north end of the valley, covering the approaches from that direction. The Confederates threatened their front with a heavy force of infantry, driving in General George Stoneman's cavalry, and Wagner made ready to receive him, covering his lines with hastily thrown-up works. The Confederates withdrew from Wagner's front after driving in the cavalry, and the night passed without incident. On May 13, the regiment ascertained that the Confederates had evacuated their works at Buzzard Roost Gap and retreated south toward the direction of Resaca. The brigade moved out in pursuit, passing through the town of Dalton and down the valley on the east side of the Chattanooga Mountain, camping near Tilton.[20]

The brigade moved out on May 14 and formed a junction at about 9:00 a.m. with General Schofield's corps, which was moving on the Confederates, who were found to been entrenched near Resaca. About midday, General Newton put his division into position on the left of the 23rd Corps, and Wagner's lines advanced to within five hundred yards of the Confederate rifle pits and artillery, the Confederate guns being protected by heavy earthworks, with an open field in front, where the Confederates shelled Wagner's brigade. After nightfall, Wagner constructed a line of works on the crest of a ridge in the open field in advance of his position, placing two regiments to support them. Wagner put two batteries of artillery in position, which opened on the Confederate works at daylight the next morning and silenced the Confederates' artillery, which had been delivering a "galling fire upon our troops the day before." On the morning of May 15, General Newton directed Wagner to relieve Colonel Sherman's brigade. A heavy fire was kept up all day between Wagner's lines and the Confederates, both being behind earthworks not more than one hundred yards apart. At about

11:00 p.m., the Confederates made an attack against Wagner's front with a heavy fire from muskets that was returned by Wagner's advance line, which held its ground. The firing was kept up for half an hour, after which the attack ceased and quiet fell on the battlefield. The Union army soon discovered that the Confederates had pulled out of their works at Resaca and had crossed the Oostenaula River.[21]

The entire division crossed the river and moved south toward Calhoun on May 16, 1863. On May 17, the brigade again took up the line of march and reached a position near Adairsville, where the Confederates were found in force, Wagner's brigade taking up a position in the rear of Sherman's, which was skirmishing heavily with the Confederates, Wagner's troops being disposed so as to cover and protect Sherman's right flank. Late in the evening, Wagner relieved Colonel Sherman's command and continued to skirmish with the Confederates until dark, suffering a loss of twenty-six men wounded. The Confederates evacuated during the night.

On May 18, the brigade continued its march, passing through Adairsville, taking the road leading to Kingston and camping by the railroad at a point four miles from Kingston. On May 19, the men continued their march, arriving at Kingston at noon. At 2:00 p.m., Wagner marched his brigade south across Two Run Creek and took position in an open field, from which the Confederates were in plain view but beyond the range of rifle fire. Wagner was ordered by Newton to move his brigade to a point one mile farther west, re-crossing the creek and taking position in an open field near the Mills. Wagner threw forward a regiment, deploying one half as skirmishers, and prepared to advance. At the same time, a brigade under General John Geary's division, of the 20th Corps, came upon Wagner's left. Wagner pushed forward and again crossed the creek just below the mills, advancing across the open field about three-fourths of a mile and massing his troops at the edge of the woods. They had remained in this position for about half an hour when Newton directed Wagner to move forward and put his brigade in line, joining his left with the right of the 20th Corps. But before he could gain this position, the lines were closed by the 1st Division, 4th Corps, forming a junction with Geary's division. By this time, night had fallen, and Wagner took a position in reserve.

On May 23, Wagner was instructed by Newton to move his brigade toward the Etowah River at Gillem's bridge, which was reached before sundown. The brigade crossed the Euharlee at Barrett's Mills, crossed Raccoon Creek by the Dallas road and camped near Burnt Hickory. A heavy rain began to fall. On May 25, the brigade moved forward toward Pumpkin Vine Creek, on the road leading to New Hope Church, where it found the 20th Corps in its advance, having met and fought the Confederates. Wagner's brigade went into position to support the 20th Corps in its front, which was engaged heavily with the Confederates. Night ended the battle. Wagner's brigade took up a position on the left of Kimball's brigade, which had connected with the left of the 20th Corps, General Harker forming on Wagner's left.

On May 26, Wagner's lines were within easy rifle range of the Confederates works, and at once he began to adjust his lines, erecting a defensive line of works in front. The skirmishing was very sharp, and the casualties began to mount. On May 27, the lines were moved forward. The skirmishers of the brigade advanced, driving in the Confederates. Heavy skirmishing was kept up while the brigade remained in its works.[22]

On June 4, the Confederates again evacuated their works, and Wagner moved from his position at New Hope Church to the left toward Morris Hill Church, six miles away. Wagner's brigade camped that night two miles from Ackworth. On June 10, 1864, Wagner's brigade formed a line of battle on General Kimball's right, confronting the Confederates, who occupied a strongly entrenched position on Pine Mountain. From June 11 through June 14, Wagner's brigade was spent skirmishing with the Confederates, while ascertaining their strength and exact positions and fortifying the ground gained by pushing the Confederates to their main works. During the night of the fourteenth, the Confederates evacuated their works, and at 4:30 a.m., Wagner's skirmishers advanced and took possession of the works. They advanced and found the Confederates entrenched in a new position. Wagner's brigade was formed in column of regiments in mass, supported by General Nathan Kimball's brigade, Harker having three regiments deployed as skirmishers in his front. They found the Rebels entrenched behind works that had been constructed for some time. Wagner threw up his own works.

The next day, Wagner advanced his lines, driving the Confederate skirmishers and throwing up barricades within rifle range of the Confederates' main works. On June 16, the Confederates evacuated their works, which Wagner occupied the next day. Wagner advanced his lines and found the Confederates again behind strongly fortified earthworks. The 97th Ohio and the 28th Kentucky were deployed as skirmishers. The 97th Ohio charged the Confederates' skirmish pits, capturing prisoners, and held its position under a heavy and continuous fire from the Confederates' main line of works during the night. The 28th Kentucky lost four men killed and twelve wounded. These two units were relieved the following morning. The 100th Illinois charged the Confederates' main line of works under a heavy rainstorm and had to wade two creeks in order to reach the works, all while under fire. The 100th Illinois succeeded in taking the works and drove the Rebels to their rear line of works. The entire line was moved up and within easy rifle range of the Confederates, who kept up a heavy fire on Wagner's lines from artillery and infantry. A constant fire was kept up by Wagner's brigade to keep the Confederates from looking over their works and away from their artillery. That night, Wagner's brigade was relieved by Kimball's brigade. The Confederates evacuated their works during the night. The Rebels were found strongly entrenched at the base of Kennesaw Mountain.[23]

On June 22, Wagner's brigade relieved Harker's brigade, throwing forward the 97th Ohio as skirmishers, who were ordered to attack on that part of the Confederate earthworks confronting his lines. They encountered the Rebels in heavy force strongly entrenched behind their works. The 97th had no protection and was shot down in heavy losses. The 97th Ohio held its ground and fortified all the ground it took during the charge. The next day, another attack was made with the 57th Indiana, throwing the 26th Ohio on its right. These two regiments moved forward and took the Rebels' rifle pits but, again, lost heavily. It was impossible to hold the captured works on the left of Wagner's lines, as the Rebels had a converging fire on the same. The 57th Indiana fell back to their former position. From June 24 through June 26, the 57th Indiana skirmished with the Rebels in front of their position at Kennesaw Mountain.

On June 27, Wagner received orders to take a position behind a portion of the works occupied by General David Stanley's division for the purpose of charging the Rebels' works. After being relieved by troops from General Thomas Wood's division, Wagner moved his command to the rear of the outer line of works occupied by Colonel Grose's brigade of General Stanley's division, and massed them in column by division—left in front, with the 40th Indiana in advance; with the 28th Kentucky following, the 100th Illinois, 26th Ohio, 97th Ohio and 57th Indiana were deployed as skirmishers. The 40th Indiana and 28th Kentucky were under Colonel John Blake of the 40th Indiana. General Charles Harker's brigade was formed on Wagner's right, leaving room to form his connection with General Kimball, who was formed to Wagner's left and rear. The skirmishers moved forward and became heavily engaged with the Confederates, and soon the entire command moved up and scaled the outer line of works.

As soon as the head of Wagner's column began crossing their works, the Confederates opened a terrific and deadly fire of artillery and musketry from their main line of works, but the blue-clad soldiers charged the works of the Rebels anyway. After several attacks on the Rebels' works, the same being defended by heavy lines of abatis as well as artillery and infantry, the command fell back for shelter to a ravine close to the Rebels' works and deployed into line. About this time, Wagner received an order that General Kimball's brigade would charge in conjunction with his, and Wagner directed the regiments in his brigade to move forward with those of Kimball's. The commands moved forward but met with such a terrific fire from the Rebels that they were compelled to fall back. In falling back, a heavy fire was poured into the right flank of Wagner's line, which meant that his right had failed to effect a dislodgement in the Confederates works and had fallen back to its main line of works—the rebels were coming out of their works and striking Wagner on the flank. After Wagner's line was repulsed in the last charge, it fell back to the main line, and Wagner received orders to return to the camp he had left in the morning, relieving those of General Wood's troops who had relieved him. Wagner's losses were 4 commissioned officers and 35 enlisted men killed and 11 commissioned officers and 165 men wounded.[24]

The Confederates evacuated their earthworks on July 2, 1864, and retreated toward the Chattahoochee River. The following day, the brigade was marched to Marietta and followed the Confederates. On July 4, the day was spent skirmishing with the Confederates, who were driven from their main works and retreated toward Atlanta. On July 9, the division marched to Roswell to take advantage of a lodgement that had been effected by the Union cavalry on the south side of the Chattahoochee River. At 5:00 p.m., the brigade was massed about one half mile northwest of Roswell, marched through the town and took a position on the bluffs on the south side. The line occupied by the brigade conformed to the top of the bluff and was partially protected by works hastily erected by the Union cavalry. That same day, the line was changed by throwing the left next to the next ridge in their front and connecting with General Kimball's brigade. In this new position, a line of works was constructed. General William Sweeny's division, of the 16th Corps, occupied the line of works. It moved out and camped near Roswell. On July 13, the brigade crossed the Chattahoochee River at Power's Ferry, where the 1st and 3rd Divisions of Wagner's Corps had already taken up position on the south side. They formed a line on the right of the division and connected with General Wood's left, having one regiment in reserve. The position was on the summit of the river bluff, commanding all the ground to the front. The brigade constructed a line of works and remained in camp for several days.[25]

On July 18, the brigade marched on the Atlanta road and camped near Buck Head. On July 19, the brigade took up a position on high ground near Peach Tree Creek. The next day, the brigade crossed Peach Tree Creek and relieved Hazen's brigade of Wood's division, which had crossed the previous day. About three hundred yards along a ridge, the Confederates skirmishers were posted in some woods, which protected them from view while they continually annoyed the brigade with their fire. At about noon, the skirmish line was advanced. The 97th Ohio and the 28th Kentucky were ordered to report to General Kimball and drove the Confederates pickets some distance, halting their line on a narrow ridge running transversely to the main Atlanta road. At this juncture, two more regiments of the brigade were moved up and sent on a reconnaissance toward the left of Wagner's skirmish line. These two regiments did not rejoin the brigade, but were entirely separated from it.[26]

The two regiments ordered to Kimball returned and formed a line of battle on the skirmish line, conforming to the crest of the ridge, the right joining to the left of the 1st Brigade and the left flank refused, there being no connection. The troops began to build works but had made little progress when the pickets were driven in; the Confederates were soon upon them. The reserve regiment was moved up, and the pioneer brigade was withdrawn and posted on the left flank in a line running perpendicular toward the rear, making the form of Wagner's line of battle nearly semicircular. In this position, the brigade repulsed repeated and desperate assaults from the Confederates, inflicting severe losses and sustaining but little injury. In the breaks between the Confederates charges, the men continued work on their defenses, and by night, they had completed a strong breastwork. The next morning, the brigade found twenty-nine Confederates dead in front of their work, many only twenty paces off. During the night, the Confederates withdrew to their main line of works, which were about three-fourths of a mile away.[27]

On July 22, the brigade advanced to within two miles of Atlanta. The Confederates had evacuated their works in their front the night before. The brigade took a position in some dense woods, about one half mile east of the main Atlanta road, and began building earthworks. The Confederates made things difficult by firing shells into these works from their fortifications around the city. The works in this position had not been completed when the brigade was relieved by a portion of General Wood's division and moved to the right as far as the Atlanta road and formed, with the right resting on the road and extending to a ravine on the left; again it began to build earthworks.

The Confederates kept up a fiery cannonade in the position, throwing shells into the works and exploding them everywhere around, killing one man and wounding four others. On July 23, the 90th Ohio was posted on the opposite side of the ravine, on its left, and built a work extending across to a second ravine. A portion of this work was later occupied by General Wood's division. The brigade continued to build earthworks and entrenchments, placing abatis and entanglements. On August 3, the skirmish line was reinforced by the 100th Illinois and advanced against the Confederate works. The Confederates opened on the advancing blue-clad soldiers with grape and shell and continued a heavy fire of artillery and rifle fire until dark, when the skirmishers were withdrawn.[28]

On August 25, plans were made for a grand attack on the Confederate earthworks. The brigade, which had been at the Buck Head and Atlanta road, was abandoned. At 11:00 p.m., the brigade moved from the left toward the right until the whole line was withdrawn. The brigade was moved to a position about three quarters of a mile in the rear of the lines built by the 20th Corps and threw up a line works, which had not yet been completed when the march was resumed; the brigade passed to the rear through General Wood's division and marched to near Utoy Post Office, where it camped for the night. The brigade moved out at 3:00 p.m. on July 27 for five miles and went into position after dark on the right of General Wood's division. The next day, the brigade was formed in a single line with one regiment in reserve between the 1st and 3rd. It built a line of works connecting with these two brigades, behind which the brigade remained until 3:00 p.m., when the command moved back about a mile on the road and turned to the east and marched about three miles in the direction of the Atlanta and Montgomery Railroad, going into position on the right of the division and joining General Kimball's left.[29]

Between August 29 and August 31, the brigade spent most of its time building earthworks. On September 1, the brigade reached the Macon and Atlanta Railroad and began to tear up and burn the tracks, later finally reaching Jonesboro. The 14th Corps and the Confederates were already in a hotly contested battle. At 4:00 p.m., the brigade formed on the left of the 1st Division in two lines, with the 57th Indiana deployed as skirmishers. The brigade immediately advanced and drove the Confederates across the two open fields about one-third of a mile each, capturing their front line of rifle pits. Darkness put an end to the advance. The night was spent building defense works and preparing for the next day's battle. The next morning, the Confederates robbed the brigade of its chance to attack the Confederates, as they had already abandoned their position. The brigade marched to Lovejoy's Station, where it found a strong line of works. The men went into position on the left of the division, connecting with General Wood's right. The brigade skirmished with the Rebels constantly until 8:00 p.m. of September 5, when it abandoned its position and withdrew to its camp near Jonesboro. On September 8, the brigade marched into Atlanta and through the town. During the four months of constant marching and fighting, the brigade lost 69 officers and 822 men, for a total of 891 men. The brigade had started out with 2,007 men. By the time the brigade reached Atlanta, the force only amounted to 1,015 men. The 28th Kentucky lost 3 officers and 78 men. Wagner gave high praise to Colonel Boone and the 28th Kentucky: "Lt. Col. Boone was wounded at Kennesaw, but refused to leave the field."[30]

The injuries Colonel J.R. Boone received at Kennesaw required him to relinquish his command for a short time to Major George Barth. For his gallantry during the Atlanta Campaign, and especially at Pine Mountain and Kennesaw Mountain, John Boone was commissioned a full colonel. He was only twenty years old.[31]

During October 28, the brigade participated in the pursuit of Confederate General John Bell Hood's army, while Union General William T. Sherman continued his March to the Sea campaign. In November, the brigade was sent back to Tennessee with the 4th Corps to engage in the campaign against Hood under Union General George Thomas.

In November 1864, General George Thomas was in command at Nashville. He advanced the 4th and 23rd Corps to Pulaski, Tennessee, to oppose the movements of Hood's army. Toward the last of the month, General Hood tried to occupy Columbia, Tennessee, but General Schofield fell back there and held it. Hood then tried to gain Schofield's rear by sending a strong force to occupy Spring Hill. Schofield was informed of this movement and sent a force of five thousand men under General Stanley to attack the Rebel army. The 28th Kentucky was with this force, under Colonel J. Rowan Boone. Spring Hill was held, and the 28th Kentucky aided in holding the position. Colonel Boone was sent forward with his regiment, with orders, to check Hood's advance on Spring Hill. He deployed his men with "great skill, and stubbornly fought the advancing Confederates, suffering serious loss, but delaying the advance until darkness came on that short November day, and the prize for which Hood was striving eluded his grasp."[32]

On November 30, the 28th Kentucky formed part of Schofield's rear guard as his army hurried on to Franklin. At Franklin, two brigades of the 4th Corps, James Lane's and Joseph Conrad's, were posted across the turnpike about one-third of a mile in front of the main line of defense. The 28th Kentucky was with Lane's brigade. It was not intended that these two brigades should make any stand in case of an assault. They were placed there to observe and to be used in the event that Hood should try to make a flank movement across the Harpeth River. By a mistake of orders, they did make a stand, and as Hood's whole army came sweeping forward in an instant, these two brigades were enveloped and compelled to fall back to the main line. They suffered serious losses. Reaching the main line with the onrushing Confederates close on their heels caused confusion, and for a little while, the key point of the line was broken. The men on the line at that place, Union General Thomas Ruger's division, 23rd Corps, and a portion of Riley's division, 23rd Corps, rallied and steadied themselves and Lane's and Conrad's men united with them. Assisted by Union General John Opdycke's brigade and other troops who were hurried to the point of danger by General J.D. Cox, commanding on the line, the defense was complete and Hood's assault failed. The Battle of Franklin turned out to be the Gettysburg of the West. Hood suffered massive losses. He lost eleven generals, six of them major generals. After the battle, the 28th Kentucky followed Schofield's army back into Nashville. Two weeks later, the 28th Kentucky would again be involved in a great battle.[33]

On December 15, at 7:00 a.m., the regiment under command of Major George Barth was formed into line of battle on the right of the front line of the 2nd Brigade, 2nd Division, 4th Corps, before the fortifications of the 3rd Brigade, 2nd Division, 4th Corps. An advance of the line was ordered, and the regiment was moved forward, conforming its movements to those of the brigade line of battle and encountering opposition from the Confederates under General Hood, who had taken up position around Nashville. The Confederates were falling back under the Union artillery and rifle fire. Just before dark, at 4:30 p.m., the Confederates were discovered preparing to stand behind a good line of works on a knoll immediately to the left of the Hillsboro Pike. The order to charge was given by the brigade's commander, Colonel Lane, and with a loud yell that "bespoke success," the regiment made their way rapidly over the stone fences, across the pike, up the hill and through the abatis. The fort, artillery and many prisoners stood as the captured "fruits of a gallant and successful charge."

The 28th Kentucky had been presented with a new flag only a few days before, and it proudly planted the flag over the fort. About a mile beyond and directly to the rear of this fort, by Colonel Lane's order, the regiment fortified its front and rested in the fort that night. Colonel J. Rowan Boone returned to his regiment on the sixteenth. The position of the regiment in the morning was the same as the previous day. The order was given to advance. Skirmishing soon broke out but did not check the advancing line. A halt was made on the hillside to the right of the Franklin Pike, and while in this position, the Confederates opened on them with a battery some distance to their right but did not cause any harm to the regiment. At 1:00 p.m., the line was again advanced, and the skirmishers soon became engaged. By 2:00 p.m., the line was fully engaged with the Rebels.

Colonel Lane ordered a charge, in which a "stirring and confident yell followed." The ground was broken and the men marched quite a span of distance, but the men went forward under the rain of grape, shell and canister and rifle fire. The 28th Kentucky drove the Confederates over the hills to the cover of a formidable line of works, covered by several heavy lines of abatis and made to secure the Franklin Pike. The brigade ran at right angles with these works, but the 28th Kentucky moved up to within easy rifle range. The 28th Kentucky was ordered to change front to the rear, and when the 28th Kentucky was shifted, it faced the Confederates in their fortifications. Skirmishers were thrown out in their front, and in a short amount of time the regiment had covered its front with a good and secure line of works from which it kept up so heavy a fire as to silence the Confederates in their front. At 4:00 p.m., the regiment was ordered to charge the Rebels' fortifications. The line was formed and the order given and received by the men, and they ran toward the works, passed the entanglements and abatis and captured many prisoners. The 28th Kentucky continued to chase the fleeing Rebels until they neared Brentwood, when darkness stopped the chase. The 28th covered the front of the brigade during the night. The regiment had fired thirty-seven thousand rounds of ammunition during the battle. Boone lost one man killed and five wounded.[34]

After the Battle of Nashville, the 28th Kentucky marched to Huntsville, Alabama, and then to Texas, where the regiment remained until December 1865. The 28th Kentucky was mustered out on January 1, 1866. When William Boone resigned from the Union army due to his poor health, he returned to Louisville to his wife, his two young children and his business affairs. After the war, he was elected to the Charter Convention of 1870. He had regained his health, but in January 1875, he was caught in a rainstorm. Typhoid pneumonia ensued, and he died on January 24, 1875. His service was held at St. Paul's Episcopal Church, and his body was taken to Cave Hill Cemetery. After the war, John Boone studied law, and in 1869, he began practice as a junior in the law firm of Boone and Boone. When his father died, John took over control of the firm. In 1870, Boone married Carrie Bell Morris, the daughter of George W. Morris, a prominent citizen and merchant of Louisville. John and Carrie had seven children: George, William P., Harney, Annie, Carrie, Fanny and Rowan Jr. John Rowan Boone died on November 28, 1883, and was buried in the same family plot as his father at Cave Hill Cemetery.[35]

Chapter 3

Union Colonel Charles Hanson

Charles Hanson was born in 1829 in Clark County, Kentucky, and was the son of Samuel Hanson, a lawyer, and the brother of Confederate General Roger Hanson of the Orphan Brigade fame. Charles was raised to be a lawyer like his father and was county attorney of Clark County until the war broke out. On October 1, 1861, Hanson took down his shingle and, unlike Roger, cast his lot with the Union. On January 6, 1862, he was mustered in at Smithland, Kentucky, and became lieutenant colonel of the 20th Kentucky Regiment of Infantry. Following the fall of Fort Donelson in February 1862, the regiment moved to Nashville with Don Carlos Buell's army, where Lieutenant Colonel Hanson was given command of the 20th Kentucky. From Nashville, they marched to Shiloh and encountered their first real taste of war.[36]

On April 6, the 20th Kentucky Infantry formed into line of battle and became heavily engaged. Hanson's regiment was assigned to the 4th Division, Brigadier General William Nelson's 22nd Brigade. The 1st Kentucky, 2nd Kentucky and 20th Kentucky were under Colonel Sanders Bruce. Hanson, in his report of the Battle of Shiloh, said that he had about three hundred men in his regiment and that the 20th Kentucky was originally slated to be held in reserve but was immediately ordered forward and to the left to support and prevent the turning of Colonel Ammne's left flank. Colonel Hanson said, "In these last three positions we were in a galling and destructive fire of the enemy's cannon and musketry. The regiment moved to them in good order, and maintained their positions with steadiness and coolness."

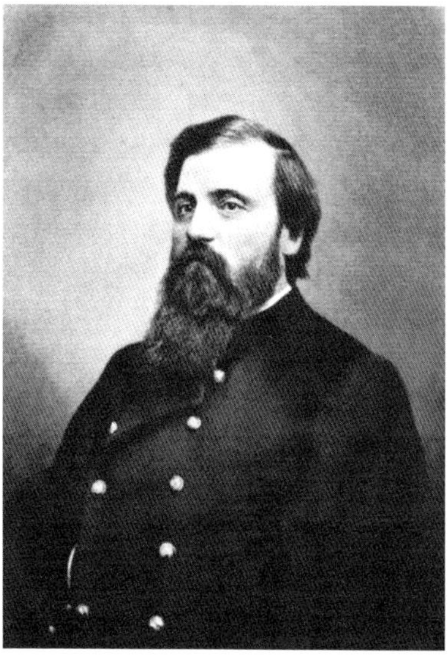

Colonel Charles Hanson. *From E. Polk Johnson's* History of the Ohio Falls Cities and Their Counties: General History with Illustrations and Biographical Sketches, *vol. 1 (1882).*

Hanson's men were assigned as skirmishers and protected the left flank. The 20th Kentucky drove the enemy from its position and secured the ground, but the Rebels quickly counterattacked. The regiment, along with four companies of the 1st Kentucky and one of the 2nd Kentucky, were to protect Captain Terrill's battery from being overrun. The 20th Kentucky, along with the battery, beat back the second attack mounted by the Confederates on the left flank, and Hanson and his regiments held on to their ground. Their last assignment at Shiloh was for them to move to the right to hold a position on the flank, but the Confederates had retreated by that time. Hanson won great praise from his other commanders. Colonel Sanders Bruce reported that Hanson's 20th Kentucky "was in full range of the enemy's fire, and at all times maintained their formation with the steadiness and tenacity becoming veterans....Hanson deserves very high commendation for the manner in which he managed his regiment at this crisis."[37]

After Shiloh, Hanson moved with the army to Corinth, Mississippi, and was involved in the Siege of Corinth, where he and his men took part in many skirmishes. On May 21, 1862, the 1st Kentucky was deployed on the left of the road leading to Corinth, with the 20th Kentucky on the right. The 1st Kentucky and 20th Kentucky were to skirmish ahead, and as soon as the skirmishers were deployed, the Confederates, who were hidden in the woods, poured volley after volley into the 20th and 1st Kentucky, driving them back to Widow Serratt's house. The enemy was trying to turn the Union left flank. Hanson was sent in with his remaining companies to the left to support the 1st Kentucky and stem the tide of gray-backs who were raining down shot and shell on his men. Artillery was brought up and fired into the Confederate ranks. The battle raged for three quarters of an hour and the Confederates rallied three times, but the Union line held firm. The 20th Kentucky pushed the enemy back and gained a position across a small creek beyond Widow Serratt's house. The Rebel fire stopped, and the Union forces held their ground until nightfall. Then Union General Don Carlos Buell recalled the 1st and 2nd Kentucky, while the 31st Indiana remained on the field to deceive the enemy into thinking that the Federals remained on the field in force. Union Colonel Thomas Sedgwick reported that Hanson "evinced the greatest bravery, gallantly leading and encouraging his men amid the greatest dangers."[38]

On May 28, Hanson was involved in a battle three-fourths of a mile beyond their entrenchments, at Corinth, Mississippi. Colonel Sedgwick reported that on the morning of May 28, the 20th Kentucky and 2nd Kentucky were formed into line of battle and made up the first line. The regiments quickly began to advance but had only gotten fifty yards or so when the Confederate forces opened up on them. The line shuddered and then slowly began to gain ground, driving the Confederates back across Bridge Creek. The bridge was hotly contested by both sides, with the Federal troops finally gaining control. Major Buckner, with two companies of the 20th Kentucky, crossed over the bridge and deployed on the left; Company B, 2nd Kentucky, and the main body of the 20th Kentucky, under Lieutenant Colonel Hanson, were ordered forward on the right. The 1st Kentucky was being driven back, and Hanson deployed his men and ordered them to fire on the Confederates. The 20th Kentucky put down such a withering and destructive fire on the Confederates that the gray-clad troops grudgingly began to fall back. Captain Mendenhall's battery rolled its guns closer to the front while the Confederate and Union troops attacked and counterattacked. The Union forces did not advance any farther than the bridge but managed to hold on to it. The Confederates finally broke off the fight, and the victorious but dog-tired Union troops began to dig rifle pits. By 9:00 p.m., the exhausted brigade had been pulled out and was given the opportunity to rest and a chance to lick their wounds. Sedgwick's report commended Colonel Hanson for "displaying great coolness and judgment both in manner of handling his regiment and in his efforts to assist me in the discharge of my duties."[39]

On May 30, Colonel Hanson's troops followed the army into an abandoned Corinth. On June 4, they pursued the enemy until they reached Baldwyn and remained there for two days. Then the 20th followed Buell's army into northern Alabama, first at Huntsville and then into McMinnville, Tennessee. In August, the regiment moved with Buell to Kentucky and marched with Union General William Nelson's Division from Louisville to Perryville. It engaged in the skirmishing of that battle on October 8 and then moved in pursuit of Bragg's army, going as far as Mount Vernon. It then marched through Somerset and Glasgow to Nashville and remained there until the month of December, when it was ordered to Bowling Green, Kentucky, guarding the railroad at various points until about the first of July, when it was sent to Lebanon, Kentucky. It just so happened that Confederate General John Hunt Morgan was headed in this same direction on his famous July 1863 raid.

Lieutenant Colonel Hanson reported that "on the morning of the 4th, instant, I received reliable information that a force, five thousand strong with six pieces of artillery, under the command of John Hunt Morgan; was approaching on the Columbia road, and that the advance was within eight miles of town." Hanson had about 360 men and no artillery. He set about trying to get horses since he had no cavalry with him. He sent out scouts, and they soon found Morgan's scouts, who were at first pushed back by Hanson's men. Then an overwhelming force under Morgan drove Hanson's men back to their pickets. Hanson encountered Morgan's scouts along the Columbia road and the Bradfordville road and, after a skirmish, pushed Morgan's men back to Muldraugh Hill. Hanson was ordered to stay and fight until reinforcements came. No fighting occurred until the next morning.

At 6:30 a.m., Hanson saw Morgan's men covering the Bradfordsville road across the Columbia Pike and the railroad to the St. Mary's road. His line stretched for nearly two miles. His position was about one and a half miles from town. Hanson threw out 280 skirmishers in a semicircle covering the front of the enemy, and about 50 more under Captain Wolcott were placed in the Bradfordsville road and to the left with directions to hold the town until overcome—they were then to take cover in two buildings on Main Street that had previously been prepared for defense and which best covered that part of Lebanon. At seven o'clock, Morgan's artillery opened up on Hanson's camp, and at the same moment, Confederate Lieutenant Colonel R.A. Alston was sent with a flag of truce. Alston demanded that Hanson surrender, but Hanson refused. Morgan then continued his shelling of the town, and his men moved to Hanson's right and left, surrounding him.

The fighting intensified. Skirmishers from the 20th Kentucky fought for two hours but finally fell back to the L&N train depot. Hanson ordered the ordnance and commissary stores destroyed. Fighting broke out in the streets of Lebanon. Hanson's men who had not reached the depot took shelter in the houses. Morgan directed his cannon to fire on the depot, and the roof soon caught on fire. With their Springfield and Enfield rifles, Hanson's men managed to keep Morgan's artillery from getting any closer than one thousand yards from the depot, but by now, the Rebels occupied about two-thirds of the town. At noon, the citizens of the town sent a flag of truce to the depot and said that if Hanson's men did not surrender in ten minutes, Morgan would burn the town to the ground. General Morgan took advantage of the ceasefire and moved his artillery to within three hundred yards and his men closer to the depot.

Colonel Hanson immediately ordered his men to fire, without giving the townsfolk any message. Morgan knew that Union reinforcements were coming, and he did not want to be caught up in a major engagement since his main objective was to reach the Ohio River. Morgan decided to storm the depot by a frontal assault. Morgan's 2nd and 5th Kentucky moved across the open ground, firing at the windows to keep the defending bluecoats down. Lieutenant Thomas Morgan, who was General John Hunt Morgan's brother, was shot through the heart during the final charge on the depot. He fell dead in the arms of another brother, Calvin. "Brother Cally, they have killed me" were his last words. At 1:20 p.m., Hanson's men were running out of ammunition, having fired 125 rounds per man. They were worn out, and most of their weapons were badly fouled. After a valiant stand lasting almost seven hours and against overwhelming odds, Lieutenant Colonel Charles S. Hanson surrendered.

When the 2nd Kentucky found out that Thomas Morgan had been killed, they were overcome by emotion and were going to kill Hanson and his men, but John Hunt Morgan, still grieving and in shock over his brother's death, rode out in front of his men and, at gunpoint, told them he would shoot anyone who tried to harm Colonel Hanson or any of his men. Laying down their arms, Colonel Hanson and his men were paroled. As he was leaving the building, Morgan turned to Hanson and said, "Charles, when you go home, if it is any source of gratification to you, tell Mother you killed brother Tom." John Hunt Morgan and Thomas Morgan knew Charles before the war, when they had been friends. Union losses were thirteen killed and twenty-eight wounded. The Confederates lost thirteen killed and thirty wounded. The three hundred captured Federals were then ordered at the double quick to Springfield.[40]

Most Civil War readers have not heard of Lieutenant Colonel Charles S. Hanson, the 20th Kentucky or the battle that took place in Lebanon, Kentucky, on a hot day in early July 1863. The Battle of Lebanon did not make the newspapers because a few of days earlier, on other battlefields far from Kentucky, the Battle of Gettysburg and Siege of Vicksburg took place, which were huge victories in the East and West for the Union.[41]

Union General Ambrose Burnside was very upset with Hanson for being paroled on the spot, telling Colonel Hanson that he should have waited until he got to City Point. Burnside put Hanson under arrest and sent him to Louisville to do provost marshal duty. Hanson objected, stating that he was a paroled prisoner and should not be forced to perform such duty. His objections were overruled, and Colonel Hanson was forced to take the post under penalty of court-martial and arrest if he refused. Major General Burnside sent Hanson to Camp Nelson without arms, where he was then given garrison duty and finally notified that he was officially exchanged.[42]

On December 29, 1863, Hanson was promoted to colonel and given a new command, the 37th Kentucky Volunteer Mounted Infantry. In March 1864, Hanson and the 37th were ordered to Columbia, Kentucky, with all available troops in the state for the purpose of moving into eastern Kentucky to pursue John Hunt Morgan and his raiders.[43]

On about June 1, 1864, Colonel Hanson's brigade was ordered to Irvine, Kentucky, to aid in checking the movement of Morgan into Kentucky. General Burbridge knew of Morgan's plans and moved to Pound Gap, but Morgan eluded him and moved on to Mount Sterling, where Hanson's Brigade skirmished with Morgan's men and lost, and then recaptured, one of Hanson's mountain howitzers.[44]

On July 12, Morgan's Cavalry, with 2,300 troopers, attacked Cynthania, Kentucky, which was defended by General Stephen Gano Burbridge and 5,000 Union cavalry. Hanson and the 37th again played a major part in the battle. Morgan's men were exhausted, and the bluecoats managed to take back prisoners that Morgan had captured at Mount Sterling. Morgan and his troopers then skedaddled for the relative safety of Virginia. In September 1864, Burbridge mounted another attack against Morgan at Saltville, Virginia, where Colonel Hanson and the 37th Kentucky fought against Morgan once more, during Burbridge's expedition to destroy the salt works.

During the battle, on October 2, 1864, Colonel Hanson was severely wounded when he was shot in the left side just above the hip. The bullet lodged in his right side after knocking off the outer part of his spine. Colonel Hanson was taken prisoner and sent to Emory and Henry Hospital in Washington County, Virginia. In a report dated October 26, 1864, surgeon W.H. Gardner, 30th Kentucky Infantry, stated:

> *On Monday morning, October 3rd…several armed men, as I believe soldiers in the Confederate service, took five men, privates, wounded (negroes), and shot them…on Friday evening, October 7th, at Emory and Henry College Hospital, Washington Co. Virginia, to which place our wounded had been removed, several armed men entered the said hospital about 10:00 P.M.*

> *and went upstairs into the rooms occupied by the Federal wounded prisoners, and shot 2 of them (negroes) dead in their beds....* [O]*n Saturday, October 8, armed men entered the hospital about 4 P.M., overpowered the guard, and shot Lt. E.C. Smith, 13th Regt. Kentucky Cavalry, dead in his bed, where he lay severely wounded. They at the same time called out for the other Federal officer's confined there, particularly Col. Hanson, 37th Regt. Kentucky Volunteers...swearing that they intended to kill all of them; and I believe that they were only prevented doing so by the exertions of Surgeon Murfree, the surgeon in charge, the steward Mr. Acres, and the other surgeons, and the hospital attendants did all in their power, even to the risk of their lives, to prevent the* [perpetration] *of these outrages; and that they assisted in removing Col. Hanson and Capt. Degenfeld, as well as myself, to a place of safety.*[45]

Colonel Hanson was transferred to College Hospital in Lynchburg, Virginia. On October 12, General Burbridge reported that Hanson had died at Emory and Henry Hospital, and on October 14, he requested Hanson's body. This was probably a surprise to Hanson, since he was still very much alive, though severely wounded.[46]

While he was held prisoner, charges were filed against Hanson by Confederate Lieutenant Colonel Alston of Morgan's command, who remembered him from the Battle of Lebanon. He charged Hanson with cruelty to Confederate prisoners and violation of his parole. Ambrose Burnside came to the defense of Colonel Hanson and wrote to Charles Dana, the assistant secretary of war, a list of statements in his defense. On November 14, G.A. Stone wrote to General Jas. H. Lane, requesting that his brother-in-law, Charles Hanson of the 37th, be exchanged. Secretary of War E.A. Hitchcock, in a letter to the assistant adjutant general, stated that he did not think that Hanson should be exchanged and that the charges against him by the Confederate government should be ignored since the Confederacy "has no legal case." The Confederates finally decided not to bring him up on charges, and as soon as he was able to be moved, they transferred him to Libby Prison in Richmond, Virginia, where he was finally paroled on March 6, 1865.[47]

After the war, Colonel Hanson returned to Kentucky and made an unsuccessful run for Congress. He then moved to Paris, Kentucky, and resided there until his death on November 8, 1875. Hanson was survived by his wife, Carrie, and his three children: Caroline W., Sarah Carter and Charles Roger. Charles Hanson was laid to rest at Winchester Cemetery,

Clark County, Kentucky. Colonel Charles S. Hanson was truly a great soldier and worthy of praise. In the November 16, 1875 issue of the *Kentucky Yeoman*, the paper declared Hanson "a fine disciplinarian, and was very popular of his soldiers. He had a great dash and decision of character.…Few men had finer social qualities, and no one better deserved the high character that he enjoyed for honor and integrity. Of a quick, active intellect, a lively, vivacious disposition and possessed of much 'Bon Hommie' and a fine sense of humor…he had great popularity. He was a brave, gallant gentlemen, and a true friend, a kind husband and affectionate father." What more can be said for this great man?[48]

Chapter 4

Union "Colonel" John Macauley

John T. Macauley was born on February 4, 1846, in Newport, Kentucky, and was the son of John and Bridget Macauley. His parents were from Belfast, Ireland, sailed to America in 1835 and were married in New York City. John was a carpenter by trade and practiced his profession for five years in New York before he moved to Cincinnati and, later, to Newport, Kentucky. When John T. Macauley was four years old, his parents moved to Buffalo, New York. Macauley continued to live in New York until the outbreak of the Civil War. John was attending Buffalo High School. Just before the Civil War erupted on the American landscape, he was one of the first to enlist in a drum corps formed by Company D, 74th Regiment, New York State Guards.[49]

When the Civil War broke out in April 1861, Macauley was only fifteen years old. He traveled to Indianapolis to be with his brother, Daniel Macauley, who joined the 11th Indiana Infantry. John Macauley became a drummer boy for the 11th.[50] Union General Lew Wallace, the author of *Ben-Hur*, trained the 11th Indiana Infantry in Zouave tactics, and it became known as Wallace's Zouaves. Daniel Macauley became first lieutenant and adjutant for the 11th Indiana Infantry.[51] The 11th Indiana was organized at Indianapolis April 21–25, 1861. The regiment moved to Cumberland, Maryland, and saw action at Romney. On July 29, it moved back to Indianapolis and mustered out on August 2, 1861. On August 31, 1861, the regiment reenlisted as a three-year regiment. On September 6, 1861, the regiment moved to Paducah, Kentucky, but on February 5, 1862, it participated in the operations against

Fort Henry and Heiman. From February 12 to 16, the regiment participated in the fight and later capture of Fort Donelson.[52]

After the Battle of Fort Donelson, the regiment participated in the Battle of Shiloh. By this time, George McGinnis had been promoted brigadier general and Daniel Macauley to regimental colonel. The 11th Indiana participated on the advance on Corinth. After the siege on Corinth, the 11th Indiana moved to Helena, Arkansas. On May 1, 1863, the regiment fought at the Battle of Port Gibson and, on May 16, at the Battle of Champion's Hill. At the Siege of Vicksburg, Daniel was wounded but recovered in time to serve with the regiment in the Department of the Gulf. The 11th Indiana camped in New Orleans until July 19, 1864, and transferred to Washington, D.C.

Daniel Macauley succeeded the brigade command, and the 11th Indiana Infantry fought at Fisher's Hill. Daniel was brevetted brigadier general for his action at the Battle of Cedar Creek.[53] John T. Macauley was promoted to sergeant major. On May 18, 1864, John T. was promoted to adjutant, and on February 26, 1865, he succeeded Captain N.R. Ruckle as commander and officer of Company C. He was mustered out of service in 1865. He then became a clerk in the office of the paymaster general at Washington, D.C. While a clerk, he went before an examination board at Baltimore, where he qualified and was commissioned captain in the 7th Regiment, Veteran Volunteers, also known as the Hancock Corps, and served as provost marshal of Loudon County, Virginia, until July 1866, when he mustered out of service.[54]

After his service in the military, he moved to Indianapolis, and in 1868, he moved to Toledo, Ohio, and embarked on a theatrical career by starting in the box office of White's Hall, the only theater in Toledo; it was under the management of his brother, Bernard. During the same year, John took over the Wood's Theater box office, located in Cincinnati, Ohio. From Cincinnati, John returned to Indianapolis and took charge of the Academy of Music, which was still under the management of his brother.

Bernard Macauley moved to Louisville and raised the funding for the Macauley Theater, which was located on the north side of Walnut, now Muhammad Ali Boulevard between Third and Fourth Street. Built by the architectural firm of McElfatrick and Sons at the cost of $200,000, the theater opened on October 18, 1873. Debts forced Bernard Macauley to sell the playhouse to his brother John. John moved to Louisville from Cincinnati in 1879. Under John's management, the theater became a huge success and hosted such actors as Sarah Bernhardt, Lily Langtry, Edwin Booth

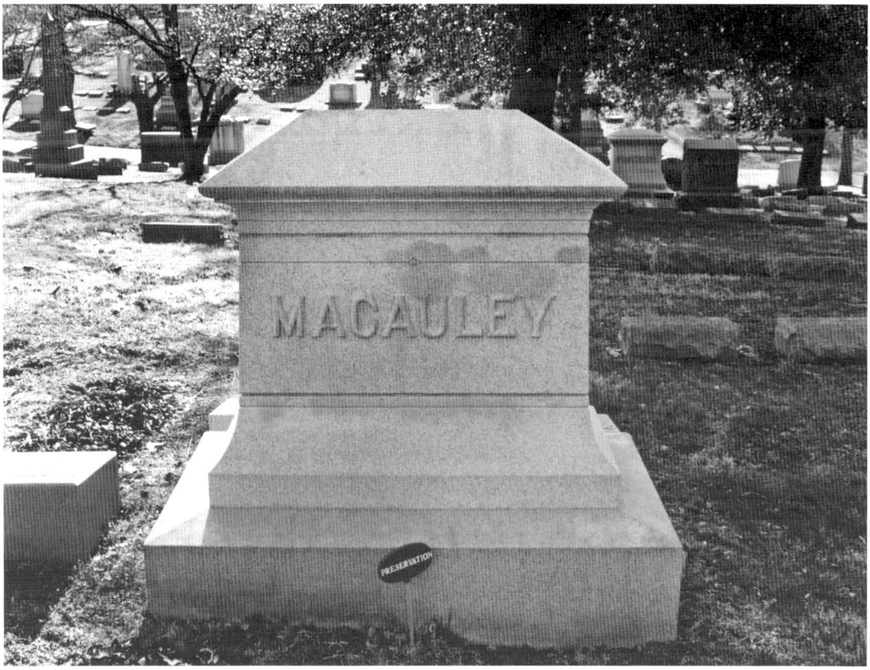

Above: "Colonel" John Macauley's grave, located in Cave Hill Cemetery. *Photograph taken by the author.*

Right: Captain John T. Macauley. *Courtesy of the Melvin Pingree Album, Northwestern University Library, Evanston, Illinois.*

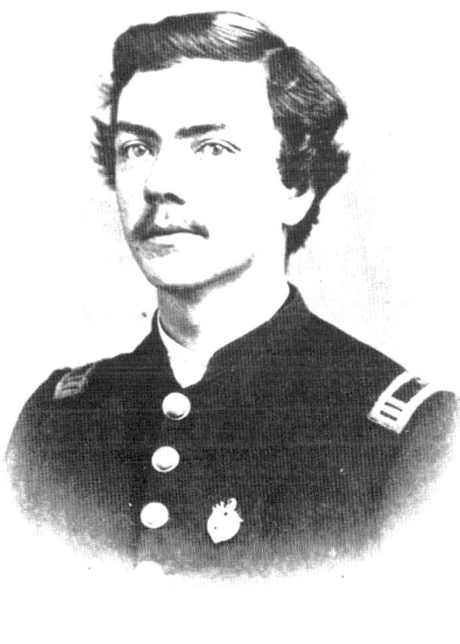

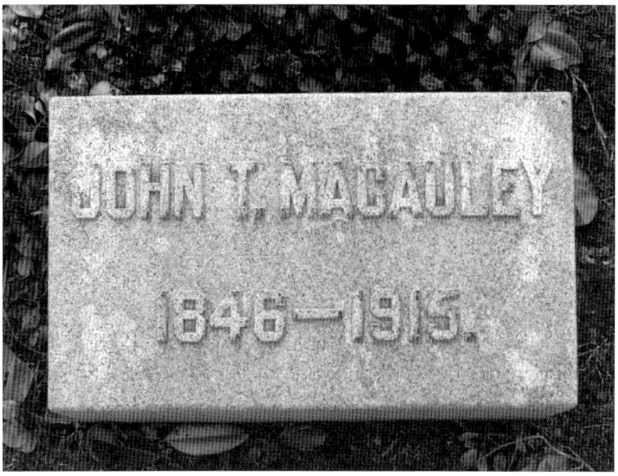

Close-up of "Colonel" John T. Macauley's headstone. *Photograph taken by the author.*

(John Wilkes Booth's brother), George Cohan and "Buffalo Bill" Cody. The Macauley Theater became Louisville's premier theater between late 1800s and early 1900s.

Macauley also founded the Chili Con Carne Club, a social organization. Members of the club included Henry Watterson and Elliott Pennebaker. One of the first acts of the club was to provide a register for the enrollment of all visitors to the clubrooms at Third and Walnut Streets. The list of names in the ledger grew to one hundred pages and listed several thousand names. Famous actors of their time such as Oliver Byron, John Drew, Fiske O'Hara, Richard Carle, Charles Hanford and Louie James filled the pages of the ledger.[55] John Macauley died on November 4, 1915, and was buried at Cave Hill Cemetery. At his funeral, his wife, Annie Macauley, along with his sisters, Mrs. Charles Pope and Sarah and Mary Kirlin, were in attendance.[56]

After his death, the theater continued to promote the city's best in theatrical performances until 1925. That year, the theater made way for the expansion of the Starks building at Fourth and Walnut Streets. The theater officially closed on August 29, 1925. The theater was succeeded by the Brown Theater on West Broadway next to the Brown Hotel. In 1972, the Brown Theater was rededicated as the Macauley Theater. In 1997, the Macauley changed its name to the W.L. Lyons Brown Theater and is today run by the Kentucky Center for the Arts.[57]

Chapter 5

Union Lieutenant Commander Charles Flusser

Charles Williamson Flusser was born on September 27, 1832, in Annapolis, Maryland, but his parents, Charles T. and Juliana Waters Flusser, moved to Kentucky when Charles Williamson was a child. In 1847, he entered the U.S. Naval Academy in Annapolis, Maryland, graduating in 1853. On July 19, 1847, he was appointed midshipman. His first cruise was made in the Cumberland River. On September 16, 1855, he was promoted to lieutenant, and in 1857, he became an assistant professor at the United States Naval Academy. From 1859 to 1860, Flusser commanded the brig *Dolphin*. When South Carolina seceded from the Union on December 20, 1860, many of Flusser's fellow officers thought that he might enlist in the Confederate army. Flusser refused an offer of a high command in the Confederate service and instead remained in the United States Navy. His two brothers, Ottokar and Guy Flusser, joined the Confederate army. Ottokar joined the 4th Texas Infantry and Guy the 4th Kentucky Cavalry.[58]

In early 1861, Charles Flusser became commandant of the Naval Academy. When the War Department worried that Maryland might join the Confederacy, Flusser was ordered to move the school's students and instructors to Newport, Rhode Island. By the fall of 1861, Flusser was no longer an instructor at the Naval Academy but rather a commander of a gunboat. He performed blockade duty off the coast of Georgia. Commodore Louis Goldborough assigned Flusser to the Burnside Expedition, and he took command of the gunboat *Commodore Perry*. He assisted in the attack of

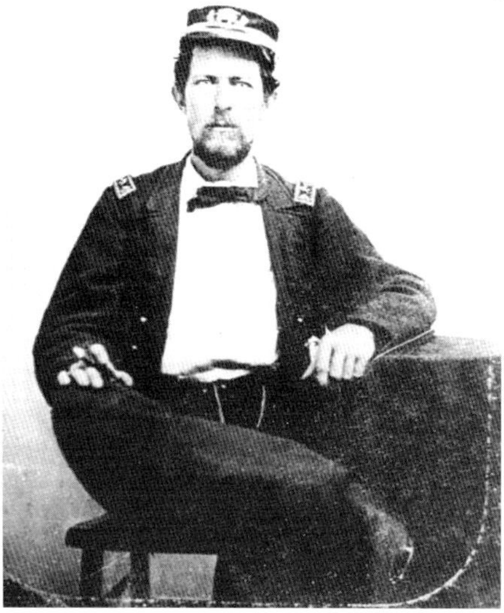

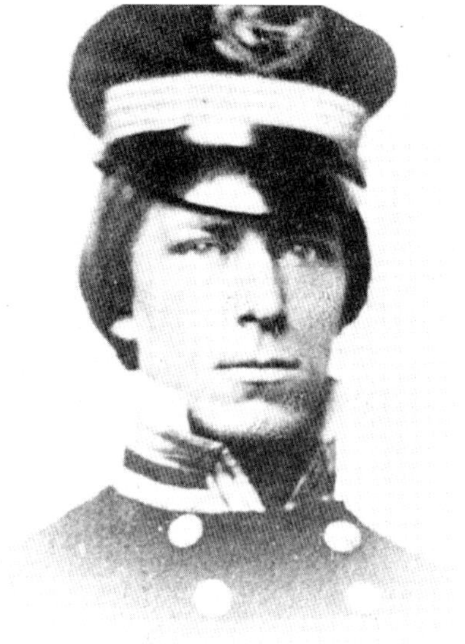

Left: Lieutenant Commander Charles Flusser. *Courtesy of the United States Naval Historical Center, Department of the Navy, Washington Navy Yard, Washington, D.C.*

Right: Midshipman Charles Flusser. This photograph was taken while he was attending the United States Naval Academy, Annapolis, Maryland. He was in the class of 1853. *Courtesy of the United States Naval Historical Center, Department of the Navy, Washington Navy Yard, Washington, D.C.*

Roanoke Island, North Carolina, which surrendered on February 8, 1862. On February 10, Flusser played a leading role in the Union victory at the Battle of Elizabeth City. He spent most of this time in the waters off the eastern coast of North Carolina and southeastern Virginia. While serving on the *Commodore Perry*, he learned of the death of his brother Ottokar at the Battle of Antietam, which occurred on September 17, 1862.

On October 3, 1862, Flusser had command of a small fleet consisting of the *Commodore Perry*, *Hunchback* and *Whitehead*. His fleet advanced up the Chowan and Blackwater Rivers to within less than a half mile of Franklin, Virginia, and twenty miles west of Suffolk. His fleet came under heavy fire from the Confederates forces that were posted on a high embankment. Flusser's fleet shelled the town of Franklin for more than three hours. He was promised the cooperation of a land force from Suffolk, but it never materialized. Without infantry support and under the threat of the capture of his ship, Flusser's fleet withdrew. He lost four men killed and seventeen wounded. Because of his actions during the Battle of Franklin, Virginia, Flusser earned the nickname of "Lion Hearted Flusser."

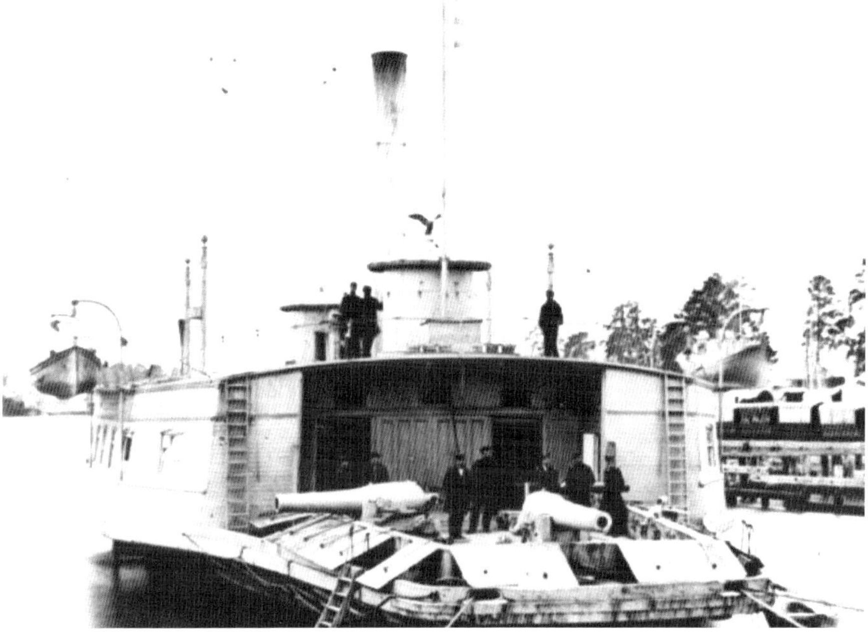

The USS *Commodore Perry*. *Courtesy of the Library of Congress.*

In May 1863, Flusser took command of the USS *Miami*, the flagship of his squadron. By April 1864, Flusser's squadron—which comprised the USS *Miami*, USS *Southfield*, USS *Whitehead* and USS *Ceres*—had been sent to Plymouth, North Carolina, to hold the Union position on the North Carolina coast. In 1862, Union forces managed to capture Plymouth and several other positions along the North Carolina coast. Union forces impeded the Confederacy at several ports of entry, which were used for blockade runners and imports of food from several different countries. In the spring of 1864, the Confederate War Department decided to try and take back the Union-held ports, including Plymouth. General George Pickett led a division to the area and launched a failed attack on New Bern in February 1864. Confederate General Robert Hoke took command and moved his army against Plymouth. He planned his attack using the CSS *Albermarle*, which was an ironclad ram that was still being built on the Roanoke River inland from Plymouth. On April 17, Hoke's 7,000 men attacked Union General Henry Wessells's 2,800 men at Plymouth. His men captured some of the outer defenses, but he needed the *Albermarle* to shell the city and the Union forts from the river. Confederate Captain James Cooke moved the *Albermarle* down the Roanoke River.[59]

When the *Albermarle* arrived at Plymouth, Cooke was confronted by Flusser's *Miami* and the *Southfield*. The *Miami* and *Southfield* were lashed together. Flusser hoped to catch the *Albermarle* between his two ships and pulverize the ram with his larger guns. He ordered his ships forward. Captain Cooke did not fall into Flusser's trap and instead decided to ram the *Southfield*. Within two minutes of the sighting, the *Albermarle* rammed the *Southfield* and fired a round that produced a huge gash in the hull, causing the ship to sink quickly. Flusser ordered both of his ships to fire their one-hundred-pound Parrott rifles and the eleven-inch Dahlgren cannons.[60]

Flusser fired the first three shots personally from the *Miami*. On the third firing, Flusser loaded the eleven-inch Dahlgren gun with a shell that had a ten-second time fuse. The shell struck the Confederate ironclad, rebounded and killed Flusser instantly, who was at the time manning the gun. A piece of the shell cut out Flusser's heart. Flusser was still holding the lanyard of his gun when his body fell on the deck of his ship. The *Southfield* sank in less than five minutes. The *Miami* cast loose, and the *Albermarle* tried to pierce the *Miami*, so the ship had no choice but to back down the river. The *Ceres* took Flusser's body to Roanoke Island.[61]

With the *Albermarle* controlling the Roanoke River, it began to fire at the Union forts. Hoke's cannons fired at the city of Plymouth and the 85th Redoubt. The Union Fort Williams and Battery Worth fired at the *Albermarle* with no effect. The cannonballs simply bounced off the hull. Hoke moved his men from Fort Gray to Wessells's right. A large Confederate force crossed the Coneby Creek below the town and massed its army on Wessells's left. On April 20, Wessells's right and front were threatened by the Confederates, advanced against his left and attacked, carrying the entire line, penetrating the town and capturing Battery Worth. General Wessells was surrounded. Confederate forces shelled Fort Williams from four different directions. At 10:00 a.m., General Wessells surrendered.[62]

During the Battle of Plymouth, the Confederates lost 163 men killed and 554 wounded but captured the entire Union garrison and a huge amount of supplies and arms. Union forces lost 150 killed and wounded, while several hundred Union soldiers eventually died at the Confederate prisoner of war camp Andersonville. When news reached the high command that Flusser had been killed in action, an outpouring of sorrow from his superior officers was communicated in the after-action reports. Major General John Peck wrote that the Union forces lost a "noble sailor and gallant patriot." General Henry W. Wessells, U.S. Army, commanding the Union forces at Plymouth, wrote that Flusser was "one of Kentucky's most noble and chivalrous sons." He added that "in the death of this accomplished sailor the Navy has lost one of its brightest ornaments and he will long be remembered by those who knew him and loved him for his intellectual worth, his social qualities and manly bearing."[63]

On June 9, 1864, Lieutenant Guy Flusser was killed at the Battle of Mount Sterling, Kentucky. His body was transported to Cave Hill Cemetery, and on July 2, 1864, he was buried on top of his brother Ottokar's empty coffin. The United States Naval Academy interred Charles Flusser's body at the military cemetery in New Bern, but in 1868, the navy transferred his remains to the U.S. Naval Academy cemetery. He is buried in Section 7, Lot 1591. Juliana Flusser was so upset at losing three of her sons during the Civil War that she erected a tombstone at the family plot and buried three coffins, each stacked on top of another. A plaque embedded in the tombstone reads, "To my sons." The official government undertaker, Washington Wyatt, buried Charles Flusser's empty coffin on April 21, 1864, in Section M, Lot 4.

Chapter 6

Union Colonel Thomas Sedgwick

"No man has exhibited more patriotic zeal and devotion to his country."

Thomas Duncan Sedgwick was born around 1837 in Louisville, Kentucky. Not much is known about his early years or even who his father and mother may have been, but on the 1860 census for Jefferson County, he was twenty-four years old and listed as a clerk. When the Civil War broke out, and Kentucky was teetering on joining the Union or the Confederacy, Sedgwick felt that he had to do something to help defend his native state of Kentucky. He helped raise a regiment, and during the war, he became a colonel for the 2nd Kentucky Infantry and eventually commanded a Union brigade. He fought in almost every battle of the Western Theater, including the Battles of Cripple Creek, Scary Creek, Bridge Creek, Shiloh, Stone's River and Chickamauga, and was present at the surrender of General Robert E. Lee to Union General Ulysses S. Grant at Appomattox.

In 1864, when President Abraham Lincoln asked for officers to command black regiments, a result of the Emancipation Proclamation, Sedgwick accepted the position as a commander of the 114th United States Colored Infantry, knowing full well that if he were caught, there would be no trial—he would be shot, and the black soldiers in his command would be taken back into bondage. Even after the Civil War ended, Sedgwick continued to serve with the 114th USCT, and he took the regiment to Brownsville, Texas, becoming part of the Buffalo Soldiers. As one of his superiors said of Sedgwick's career, it was one of "patriotic seal and devotion to his country."

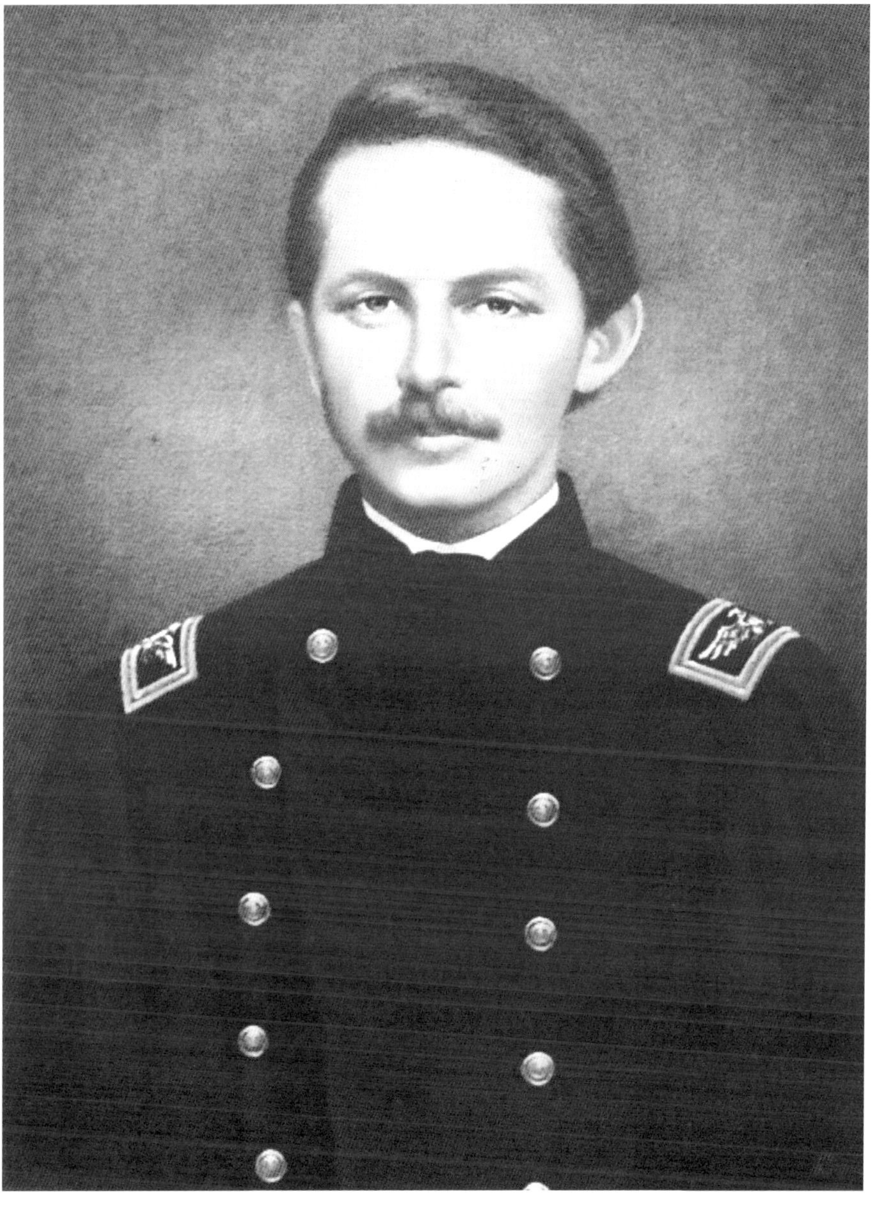

Colonel Thomas Sedgwick. *Courtesy of the Old Bardstown Village Inc. Photograph taken by the author.*

On April 12, 1861, the Civil War began when Confederate General P.G.T. Beauregard fired on Fort Sumter in the Charleston, South Carolina harbor. Several days later, on April 17, 1861, Louisville, Kentucky, hoping to remain neutral during the conflict, spent $50,000 for the defense of the city, but Louisville citizens began to choose sides. On April 20, two companies from Louisville, under the command of Captain Ben Anderson and Fred Van Alstine, left for New Orleans and were later joined by Captain Jack Thompson's company. On April 25, Captain Joe Desha and one hundred men from Harrison County, along with three companies from Louisville under Captain John Pope, J.B. Harvey and Michael Lapielle, left the state to join the Confederacy.[64] According to Thomas Sedgwick, Louisville, Kentucky, was "thronged with Rebel soldiery and their recruiting officers, and rendezvous were on every street, with the Southern flag flaunting therefrom."[65]

During the early months of the war, Kentucky politicians had not officially declared whether the state would fight for the Confederacy or the Union. Kentucky's neutrality sent the state into mass confusion, with Union and Confederate regiments sometimes being raised on the same streets. Many of Thomas Sedgwick's friends tried to persuade him to join the Confederacy, but he was a loyal Unionist. Sedgwick felt that something must be done in Louisville to support the Union. He decided to raise a company for the

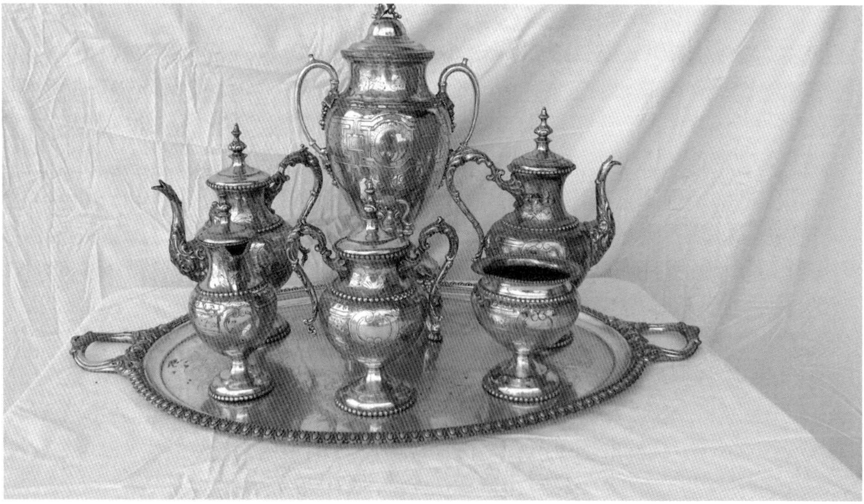

Colonel Thomas Sedgwick's silver tea and coffee set, presented to him by the men of the 2nd Kentucky Union Infantry. *Courtesy of the Old Bardstown Village Inc. Photograph taken by the author.*

Union army. He knew that it "would be a difficult and dangerous task…I was fearful to breathe my project to anyone."[66]

With the help of the Union League, men like William Woodruff, Lovell Rousseau and Thomas Sedgwick began to form companies for the defense of Louisville, Kentucky, but since Kentucky remained neutral, Sedgwick was forced to recruit troops outside the state. According to Sedgwick, Confederates learned of his plans to recruit a regiment, and he was forced to leave his home at night and cross the river into Indiana. He was "branded as a traitor and abolitionist."[67] His family residing in Louisville were forced to give up their home and move to Indiana. Rousseau established Camp Joe Holt, located in the state of Indiana, opposite Louisville, and Camp Clay was established on the Ohio side of the river opposite Newport, Kentucky. Woodruff took two infantry companies from Louisville to Camp Clay, including twenty-four-year-old Thomas D. Sedgwick. On June 3, 1861, Sedgwick became captain of Company B, 2nd Kentucky Infantry.

Several days later, on June 10, 1861, Sedgwick was promoted to major of Company B, and on June 13, 1861, the 2nd Kentucky Volunteer Infantry was mustered into service. On July 9, 1861, Sedgwick and the 2nd Kentucky, along with the 1st Kentucky Infantry, left Camp Dennison, Ohio, for West Virginia. The two regiments traveled by boat, landed at Guyandote and marched to Barbourville. The regiment joined Brigadier General Jacob Cox on the

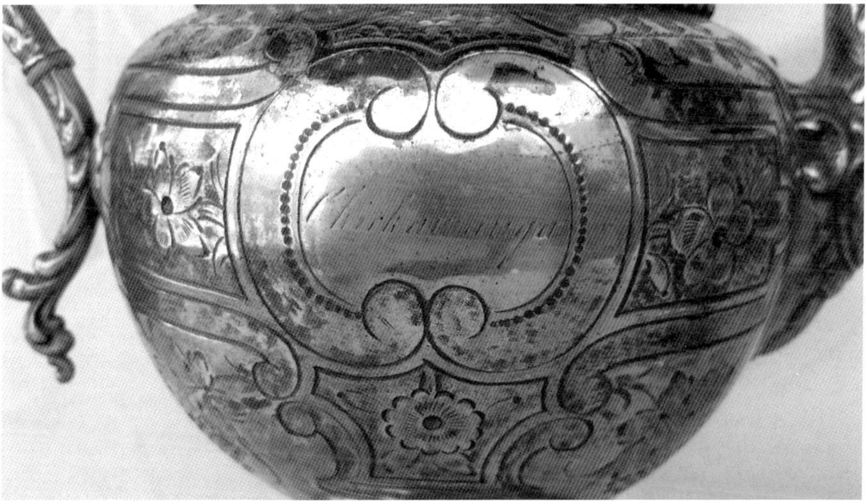

Each piece of Colonel Sedgwick's silver tea and coffee set is engraved with a battle honor, such as for Chickamauga. *Courtesy of the Old Bardstown Village Inc. Photograph taken by the author.*

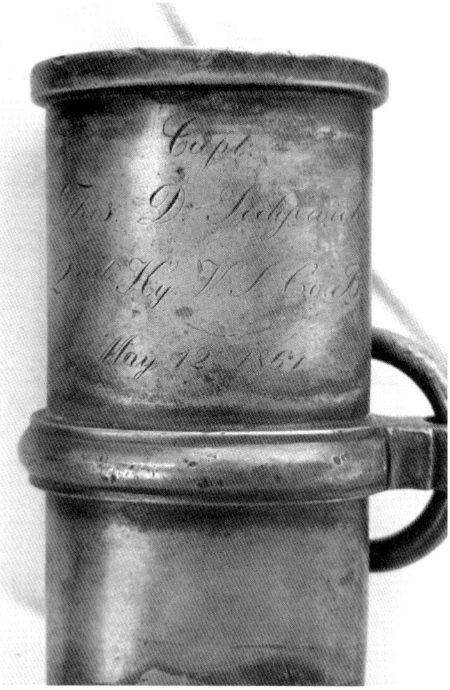

Left: Captain Thomas Sedgwick's presentation sword, given to him by his men of the 2nd Kentucky Infantry on May 12, 1861. The engraving is on Sedgwick's scabbard. *Courtesy of the Old Bardstown Village Inc. Photograph taken by the author.*

Below: Captain Thomas Sedgwick's presentation sword and scabbard. *Courtesy of the Old Bardstown Village Inc. Photograph taken by the author.*

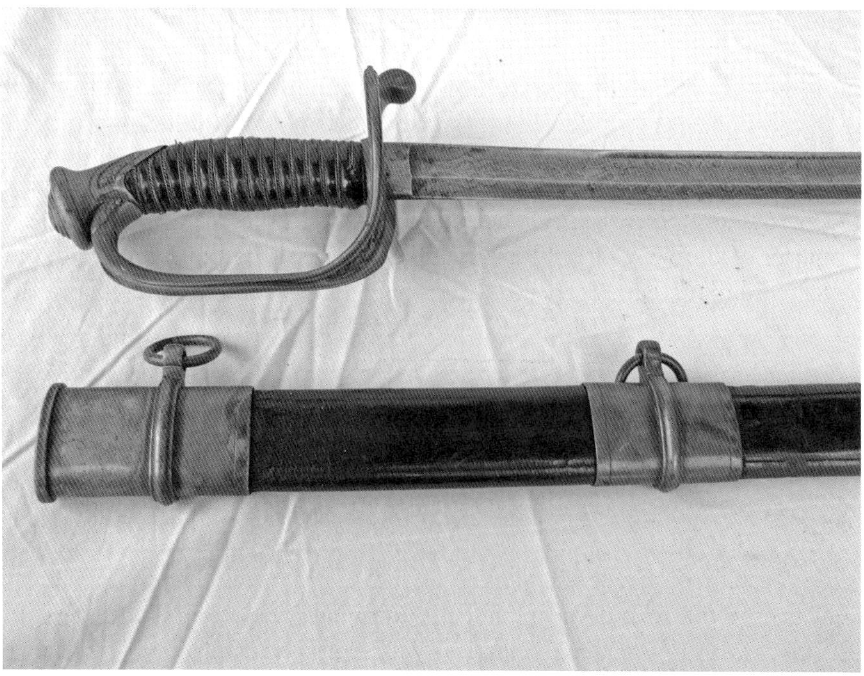

Kanawha River. On July 17, 1861, the 2nd Kentucky fought at the Battle of Scary Creek. Confederate infantry under the command of Colonel Albert Jenkins, 22nd Virginia, captured Colonel William Woodruff, commander of the 2nd Kentucky, along with the lieutenant colonel and two of the captains when they rode outside the Union picket line and right into Captain Jenkins. With most of the commanders of the 2nd Kentucky captured, the command devolved onto Sedgwick. At the age of twenty-four, Sedgwick became commander of one thousand men, who had untrained officers and little experience. Sedgwick said that he felt "unfitted for the command, and insisted upon the appointment of someone more competent."[68]

On July 25, 1861, the 1st and 2nd Kentucky, 11th and 12th Ohio and some regiments of militia were organized into the Brigade of the Kanawha, under General Jacob Cox. For seven months, Sedgwick and the 2nd Kentucky participated in the Kanawha Valley Campaign under Generals William Rosecrans and Cox. The 2nd Kentucky participated in many engagements, including the Battle of Gauley Bridge and Cotton Hill.

On January 25, 1862, the 2nd Kentucky reported to Union General Don Carlos Buell at Louisville, Kentucky. While in Louisville, Buell appointed Sedgwick a colonel, and the 2nd Kentucky became part of the 22nd Brigade, under Colonel Sanders Bruce. Once in Kentucky, the 2nd Kentucky marched to Bardstown and from there to the Green River. It continued to follow evacuating Confederate troops under Albert Sidney Johnston from Kentucky into Tennessee.

At the Battle of Shiloh, on April 7, 1862, between 9:00 a.m. and 10:00 a.m., General William Nelson ordered the 2nd Kentucky to move forward and attack a Confederate battery that was shelling the left wing. After advancing for about a quarter of a mile, Colonel Sedgwick found himself perpendicular with the battery. He immediately ordered a change of front to the rear, but before the movement was completed, Rebel regiments hiding in a dense thicket opened fire. Sedgwick's men and officers were caught off guard but soon rallied and advanced, supported on the right and left by two regiments. When the 2nd Kentucky approached the edge of a thicket, the fight became almost hand to hand. Sedgwick said the "slaughter on both sides was terrible."[69] Within thirty yards, more than two hundred Confederates fell from Union fire. The 2nd Kentucky drove the Rebels from the thicket, but they rallied around the battery stationed on a small hill directly in front of them. The 2nd Kentucky went up the hill with a cheer and in ten minutes had taken the battery. It held the battery for only a few minutes. Two additional Confederate regiments advanced on the 2nd Kentucky and forced it to fall back.[70]

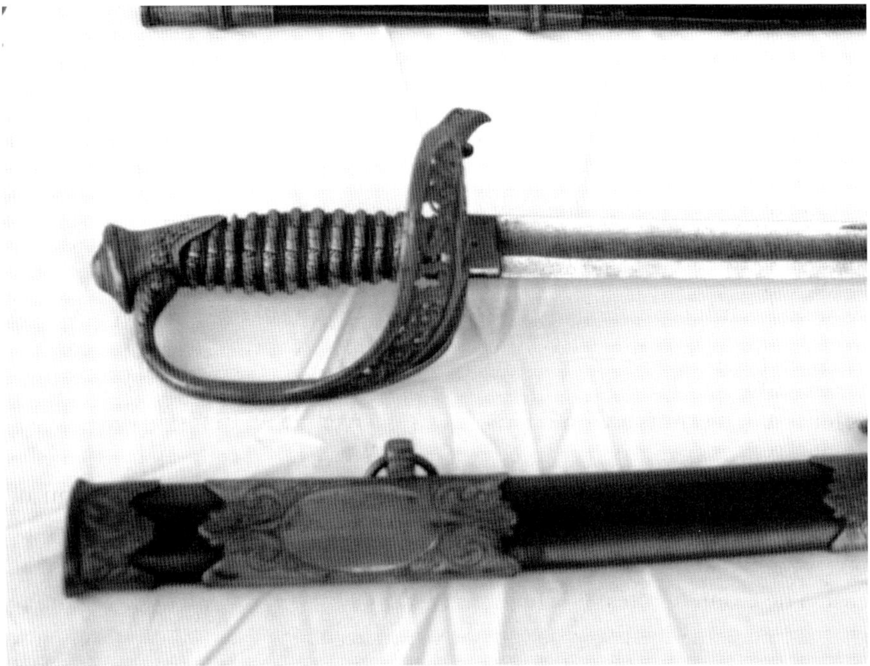

Colonel Thomas Sedgwick's second presentation sword, given to him by his men. The sword has battle honors on bronze medallions affixed to the leather scabbard. *Courtesy of the Old Bardstown Village Inc. Photograph taken by the author.*

While retiring from the field, the Confederates charged and tried to take the colors of the 2nd Kentucky, but the regiment managed to hold on to its flag, although it was riddled with holes from grape and musket balls. After the 2nd Kentucky managed to rally, General Don Carlos Buell ordered the regiment to support a Union battery that had engaged a Confederate battery. The 2nd Kentucky, along with a portion of Colonel Cyrus Dunham's 50th Indiana Infantry, charged the Confederate battery, routing it completely and securing its guns. Sedgwick had to personally run one of the captured Rebel guns to the rear and spike it, while the rest of the cannons were turned on the Confederates' cavalry, who were seen retreating through the woods on the Union right. The 2nd Kentucky remained on the spot until several regiments joined it and then withdrew, joining its brigade. During the battle, Sedgwick was wounded by a spent canister shot. In the after-action report on the Battle of Shiloh Colonel Sanders Bruce reported that during the battle "Col. Sedgwick…displayed the greatest courage and daring."[71]

After the Battle of Shiloh, the 22nd Brigade camped on the field and later moved three and a half miles from Pittsburgh's Landing. On April 14, 1862, Sedgwick took command of the 22nd Brigade. On May 2, the brigade moved ten miles and advanced on the Hamburg and Corinth Road. From May 7 to May 27, the 2nd Kentucky moved toward Corinth, Mississippi, building roads and trenches. On May 28, Colonel Sedgwick moved his brigade forward and proceeded fifty yards before they were opened on by the Confederate pickets, who were posted in a thicket on their left and in a dense wood and swamp in front of their right. Sedgwick's skirmishers advanced slowly, pushing the Confederates back to Bridge Creek. Two companies from the 20th Kentucky and Company B of the 2nd Kentucky engaged the enemy. After a half hour, the Confederates were driven back about fifty yards and regained possession of the main road leading from Farmington to Corinth. The two companies advanced under heavy fire and gained possession of the bridge, with the Confederates taking up position some fifty yards on the opposite side of Bridge Creek. Sedgwick ordered for the bridge to held at all cost. The Confederates reformed and advanced, with the intent of regaining possession of the bridge. The Confederates fired into the ranks of Company B, but the men returned fire, causing the Confederates to fall back.

In the meantime, the 20th Kentucky was ordered across an open field on the right, some five hundred yards from the bridge, and took position in the woods and swamps to support the skirmishers of the 1st Kentucky

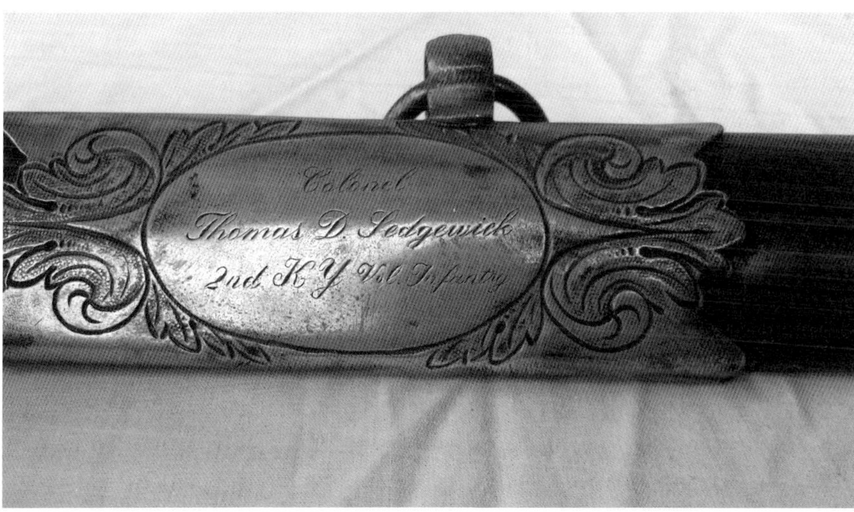

Close-up of Colonel Thomas Sedgwick's presentation sword. *Courtesy of the Old Bardstown Village Inc. Photograph taken by the author.*

Infantry. The Confederates were gradually driving the Union skirmishers back when Colonel Charles Hanson of the 20th Kentucky opened fire on the Confederates and drove them back. During this time, Colonel Sedgwick ordered the brigade and Captain John Mendenhall's battery to take position. The 2nd Kentucky was ordered to support the forces engaged at the bridge. The 1st Kentucky was to support the battery.

The intensity of the fight at the bridge began to increase, and the Confederates were trying to turn Sedgwick's left flank. He immediately ordered the 31st Indiana to reinforce his position. Sedgwick personally rode forward to the front and ordered Captain Mendenhall to open his batteries up on the enemy. After a few shells, the Confederates broke and retreated in disorder; Sedgwick's men, with cheers and yells, chased the fleeing Confederates. The Union troops had run after the fleeing Confederates for only a short distance when the Confederate batteries opened on them with grape and canister, stopping them and forcing them to return to their position. The Confederates reappeared and advanced, arriving only fifty yards from Sedgwick's position. The Confederates poured volley after volley into his ranks, but the attack was repelled. Sedgwick reported that it was "here the heroic bravery of our Kentucky troops, supported with equal courage to those of our sister state [Indiana], proved more than a match for the boasted chivalry of Louisiana."[72] Sedgwick was now up against six thousand Rebel infantry and ordered his battery to again open fire. The Confederates began retreating, "leaving us masters of the hard earned bridge."[73]

At 9:00 p.m., Sedgwick along with ten companies began to reinforce the position by building rifle pits. By daylight, the entire front line had been marked with rifle pits. At 5:00 a.m., the brigade was relieved by the 19th Brigade.

After the Confederates had fled Corinth, Mississippi, the brigade, under Colonel Sedgwick, marched to Athens, Georgia, and then on to Murfreesboro, Tennessee. On August 13, 1862, the brigade was moved to Lavergne and to Murfreesboro on August 22. From September to October 1862, the 2nd Kentucky marched with Union General Don Carlos Buell's army to Kentucky. From Kentucky, the 2nd Kentucky returned to Tennessee.

When Colonel William Woodruff was exchanged on April 4, 1862, he wanted his old command back and petitioned for the 2nd Kentucky. The petition for Woodruff's return to his old regiment made Colonel Sedgwick uncomfortable since he was in command of the regiment. On November 12, 1862, Colonel Sedgwick wrote to the secretary of war pointing out the General Order No. 102, which stated, "All captive officers should be transferred to skeleton regiments and all vacancies thus occasioned in Volunteer regiments be filled by the Governors of their respective states"—also, on January 25, 1862, the governor of Kentucky had appointed him colonel of the regiment. He made note that he had now been in command of the regiment for sixteen months but that he was willing to give up the regiment if it was necessary and "cheerfully relinquish" his position for Colonel Woodruff, "as I would desire to see him retain the fine command he has at present."[74] But Sedgwick also said that he did not want to lose his job and be kicked out of the service just because he "obeyed orders and filled the vacancy." The issue was finally settled when the secretary of war made Colonel Woodruff commander of the 3rd Brigade, 1st Division, Army of the Cumberland, and Sedgwick stayed in command of the 2nd Kentucky.

On December 26, 1862 the 1st Brigade, composed of the 2nd Kentucky Infantry and the 31st Indiana Infantry, left its camp in Nashville, marched along the road and arrived within one mile of La Vergne but halted when it met resistance from Confederate artillery and infantry. The Union cavalry and several regiments of infantry were sent forward and drove the enemy back. The next morning, the 2nd Kentucky marched until it reached Stewart's Creek. On December 29, the 2nd Kentucky and the 31st Indiana marched toward Murfreesboro. That night, the regiment camped three miles from Murfreesboro, and in the morning, it took a position about half a mile to the right of the pike. The two regiments were thrown forward in extreme advance of the division, in a cedar wood, confronting an expensive open field, in which the Rebels had two rows of rifle pits and two batteries.

On Colonel Sedgwick's right, his front-line skirmishers were supported by General James Negley's division and by Colonel William Grose, commanding the 3rd Brigade of the division, on his right. On December 31, the entire line of General James Negley, on Colonel Sedgwick's right, became heavily engaged. Colonel Sedgwick was given the order to advance and pushed the Rebels from the crest of a hill in front of them. The front line of the brigade moved forward to the fence line at the edge of the woods and at the foot of the hill. The skirmishers and front line of General Negley's division had fallen back to the rear, and those on the left had come to a halt and were engaged two hundred yards in Colonel Sedgwick's rear.[75]

By this time, the Confederates had emerged from the woods in their front and on the right and advanced in column, driving Colonel Sedgwick's skirmishers back to the front line. The Confederates reached the crest of the hill toward Colonel Sedgwick's front, halted and delivered a well-directed volley on his regiment. Captain William Standart's battery immediately on his right and Colonel Sedgwick's two regiments in front simultaneously opened up on the Rebels. Sedgwick's fire broke the Rebels' front line, and it began to fall back. Another line was forced up to the same position but was also sent to the rear, and another Rebel unit was advanced and planted its colors in the ground and then extended its line, deploying to the right and left. The entire Rebel line threw itself on the ground and at once opened up on Colonel Sedgwick, keeping up "a murderous fire."[76] General Charles Cruft ordered Colonel Sedgwick's regiment to the left. He found that his support on the left had fallen back to a point near half a mile in the rear and farther to the left. He also discovered that General James Negley's entire line had given way and that his troops, artillery and infantry were hurrying through the woods to the rear, leaving the entire Union right flank exposed and unprotected.

The Confederates had driven back the brigade on Colonel Sedgwick's left and gained possession of the high grounds around a burned house. They had also posted a battery, with one section turned on Colonel Sedgwick's position and its guns "hurling with fearful accuracy perfect showers of grape and shell."[77] On the right, the Rebels had pressed closely on the retiring forces of General Negley and had gained a point within 150 yards of Colonel Sedgwick's position, when Captain Standart, wheeling one section of his battery to the right, opened up on the Rebels with such effect that they were stopped—nonetheless, they immediately opened up on his position with "a terrible fire of musketry."[78]

The Confederate batteries and infantry in front of Colonel Sedgwick kept up an incessant firing, leaving Colonel Sedgwick's position exposed to the fire of artillery and musketry, but his men stood up nobly, preventing several different attempts to gain their position from the front. For more than two hours, the 2nd Kentucky and the 31st Indiana held their positions at the fence but nearly exhausted their ammunition. Colonel Sedgwick informed General Cruft of his situation and asked to withdraw. He refused, saying that the 2nd Kentucky and the 31st Indiana must hold their position in order to protect the retreat of General James Negley's artillery. Colonel Sedgwick relieved the 2nd Kentucky at the fence with the 90th Ohio, and the 31st Indiana was relieved by the 1st Kentucky Infantry.

By the time the line had been formed at the fence, the Confederates, reinforced and advanced, approached Colonel Sedgwick's flanks and toward his front eight Confederate columns headed toward him. The 1st Kentucky jumped over the fence and advanced to meet the Rebels but was forced to fall back under the oncoming columns of Confederates. The 1st Kentucky and the 90th Ohio kept the Rebels in check, but when Colonel Sedgwick returned to the rear, he found that all efforts to obtain a fresh supply of ammunition for the 2nd Kentucky and the 31st Indiana were nonexistent. Again Colonel Sedgwick informed General Cruft of the facts. General Cruft sent Colonel Sedgwick to ascertain the situation on the left and in the rear. He found the 2nd Brigade holding its ground in the rear and one brigade of Negley's division facing immediately to their rear and firing at the Rebels, who were advancing in that direction. Colonel Sedgwick reported back to General Cruft, who gave the order for the brigade to fall back slowly.

After returning through the woods about two hundred yards, Colonel Sedgwick took command of his regiment and advanced, but with little support and the Rebels advancing in large numbers, he decided to withdraw and rejoin the brigade. While withdrawing, Colonel Sedgwick was informed that three pieces of artillery belonging to General James Negley's division had been abandoned in the woods four hundred yards to his right and were about the fall into the hands of the Rebels. Colonel Sedgwick immediately moved his regiment by the flank double-quick to the cannons and removed them. After gaining possession of the cannons, he rejoined the brigade, which was formed on the railroad.[79]

The next morning, the 2nd Kentucky moved with the brigade to a position farther to the left, near Stone's River, to support Captain George Swallow's 7th Indiana battery. Colonel Sedgwick ordered his men to build small breastworks in their front, around the guns of the battery, and remained in an exposed position. The Battle of Murfreesboro was over. The 2nd Kentucky lost seventy-seven men. Colonel Charles Cruft said, "Colonel Sedgwick displayed marked gallantry on the field."

On January 30, 1863, the 2nd Kentucky was still in General Charles Cruft's brigade, of General John Palmer's division, General Thomas Crittenden's corps. The 2nd Kentucky remained in Murfreesboro until May. Between June and July 1863, the 2nd Kentucky stayed in Manchester. In August, they marched to Dunlap, and in September, they marched to Chattanooga, Tennessee.

At the Battle of Chickamauga, on the morning of September 18, 1863, the 2nd Kentucky Infantry moved with its brigade to Gordon's Mills. That morning, heavy firing opened on its front, and the 2nd Kentucky moved forward. It moved down the Rossville road and, after a mile and a half, went into position. The order was given for the division to advance by brigades. General William Hazen's 2nd Brigade was on the left, General Cruft's 1st Brigade was in the center and Colonel William Grose's 3rd Brigade was on the right. Colonel Sedgwick's regiment was on the right of the 1st Brigade. The 2nd Kentucky had advanced four hundred yards when Sedgwick's skirmishers became engaged with the enemy. They pushed the Confederates back, and the order was given for the brigade to halt. The 2nd Kentucky was on low ground and exposed to enemy fire from three sides. Two captains were wounded and nine men killed and wounded. Colonel Sedgwick rectified the alignment and opened fire on the Confederates, driving them back to the first line, but the Confederates were reinforced and Colonel Sedgwick was forced to halt, although he still maintained his ground. Colonel Grose's brigade had not joined Colonel Sedgwick on the right, leaving him exposed to an enfilading fire and forcing him to turn his flank. His men were falling fast. Luckily, the 23rd Kentucky, of Grose's brigade, came up and was able to hold back the Confederates. The Confederates kept up their fire for one and a half hours, at which time their left was repulsed and they began to withdraw, moving to the right.[80]

After a short time, fire was opened on the 2nd Kentucky's right, sweeping around to Colonel Grose's brigade, which formed on Colonel Sedgwick's right and occupied a ridge. Colonel Sedgwick changed his front perpendicularly to the rear, as he was moving his troops into position, when Union soldiers began to fall back in disorder. Colonel Sedgwick was forced to fall back two hundred yards. The regiment rallied and re-formed to face the oncoming Confederates. The enemy halted and retired behind a hill. Colonel Sedgwick's command was far in advance, separated from the remainder of the brigade and without support, but luckily, General John Turchin's brigade moved up in support on the left and a battery was placed in front of Sedgwick's regiment. He was also joined by the remaining regiments of the 1st Brigade. The Confederates withdrew, and the order was given to retire.

The next morning, on September 20, Colonel Sedgwick ordered his men to build a temporary breastwork. His position was on the left of the front line of the brigade, connected with the right of General Richard Johnson's division, and the 31st Indiana was up on his right. At 7:40 a.m., Colonel Sedgwick's skirmishers became engaged and were driven in. The Confederates advanced on his breastworks. Their first line was driven back, but again and again they advanced, and each time they were repulsed. At 11:00 a.m., the firing on both sides gradually ceased. Colonel Sedgwick was relieved by the 90th Ohio. Colonel Sedgwick moved back about one hundred yards and took position on a crest. At 5:00 p.m., Sedgwick realized that the right on the Union line was giving way, and the order was given to retire.

He moved about one hundred yards by the flank, entering a large cornfield. While moving into the cornfield, he was hit with the fire of musketry and artillery. They retired across the field, maintaining their position in the brigade. They continued to retreat for Rossville. Colonel Sedgwick said of his men, "I had never seen men act more coolly or deliberately, or obey more properly under any circumstances."[81] For his conduct in the Battle of Chickamauga, Colonel Sedgwick was recommended by his superior officers for promotion.

During the month of November, Colonel Sedgwick was ordered to guard the line of the Tennessee River and was placed in command of the 1st Brigade, consisting of nine regiments and a battery, and ordered to hold and guard the post at Bridgeport, Alabama, and the bridges there. He did this for several weeks, until relieved by Brigadier General Charles Cruft, the permanent commander.

In May 1864, the Military Board of Commission charged Sedgwick with "[g]iving duplicate discharges to enlisted men in violation of paragraph 165, Revised Army Regulations." According to the board, Sedgwick gave a duplicate discharge to Private Alfred S. Homer, a member of the 2nd Kentucky Infantry, which carried the penalty of dismissal. In his defense, Colonel Sedgwick said that his only recollection "is that Albert Homer was discharged to allow him to enter the Navy." He could not conceive how the error was committed and noted that the duplicate was simply an error in judgment, "committed without any criminal motive what so ever." On May 12, 1864, the board did not "exonerate him from censure, but in consideration of his valuable services and excellent testimonials as a brave and efficient officer, the Military Board of Commission recommended his exemption from dismissal."

After the Battle of Chickamauga, the 2nd Kentucky participated in the Siege of Chattanooga and the reopening of the Tennessee River. By 1864, the 2nd Kentucky was marching to Tunnel Hill, Buzzard Roost Gap and Rocky Face Ridge. On June 2, the 2nd Kentucky arrived at Resaca, Georgia. On June 3, the regiment had operations against Confederate General John Hunt Morgan. On June 19, 1864, the 2nd Kentucky was mustered out.

On June 2, 1864, Major W.H. Sidell, command of the 15th U.S. Infantry, wrote to Major General James Fry, provost marshal general, State of Kentucky, asking that Sedgwick be retained for three months at Camp Nelson, because he is "doing such important service in connection with negro recruiting….The service of Colonel Sedgwick is performing now is to attend to the enlistment of a great number of negro slaves at Camp Nelson— six hundred reported yesterday and more coming in hourly and I have no other fit officers for the purpose."[82] On July 3, 1864, Colonel Sedgwick was relieved from command of the 2nd Kentucky Infantry and was appointed by the president of the United States as colonel of the 114th United States Colored Infantry, stationed at Camp Nelson, Kentucky. Camp Nelson was the third-largest black recruiting center in the United States. In March 1865, Sedgwick and the 114th U.S. Colored Infantry were transferred to Virginia. From March to June 1865, he was assigned to command the 2nd Brigade, 1st Division, 25th Army Corps. On April 9, 1865, Colonel Sedgwick and the 114th U.S. Colored Infantry were present at the surrender of General Robert E. Lee to Union General Ulysses S. Grant at Appomattox Court House.

With the Civil War ending in April with the surrender of Confederate Generals Robert E. Lee and Joseph Johnston, the Federal government on June 30, 1865, sent Colonel Sedgwick on board the steamship *De Moley* and transported him to Brownsville, Texas. From July 1865 to December 1866, he was in command of the 114th USCT at Brownsville, Texas. By October 1866, Sedgwick had become a brevet brigadier general.

On December 31, 1866, Sedgwick was arrested. The reason is extremely unclear, even to Colonel Sedgwick. He wrote to Major General George Hartsuff, assistant adjutant general, Department of the Gulf, that Special Order No. 90, Extract 4, which placed him under arrest, did not specify any charges: "No charges have been received as yet by me." According to the records, Sedgwick took horses from the local civilians to mount his men. He gave the locals vouchers for the horses without securing permission from the government, but Sedgwick pleaded his case, along with affidavits from such generals as Philip Sheridan, and finally was released from arrest in January 1867. He returned to Texas to command the 114th USCT, and in April 1867, he was sent to Brazos Station, Texas. Sedgwick was finally discharged honorably on April 2, 1867.

On April 26, 1879, the *New York Times* reported that Sedgwick walked into the Chambers Street Hospital and asked to have a slight scalp wound on the back of his head dressed. He claimed that the wound came from a fall in the street during a fit. According to the paper, he smelled of liquor and appeared to have just finished a prolonged binge. Sedgwick told the hospital that he never had a fit before and declined to remain at the hospital after his wound had been dressed, saying that he would go to the Park House, where he was stopping. Forty-five minutes later, the Broadway squad of police found Sedgwick lying on one of the benches, dead. Sergeant Gray of the Twenty-Fifth Precinct searched Sedgwick's body but found nothing except a pocketbook containing a slip cut from a newspaper referring to the Sedgwick estate. The proprietor of the Park House said that he had not seen Sedgwick in a few days and was amazed to learn that he was dead.

Sedgwick had arrived at the Park House on April 18. He had a satchel with him but was gone from the room. An envelope found on the washstand in the room was postmarked to "Colonel Thomas D. Sedgwick, Tenth Street, N.W. Washington, D.C." The address had been scratched out with a lead pencil, and the address 354 Pennsylvania Avenue had been written with a blue crayon in one corner of the envelope. On the envelope was stamped "Superintendent of Construction, United States Government Buildings." The contents of the envelope contained a circular from the Union Republican Congressional Executive Committee, August 9, 1875, and was addressed to "Sedgwick, Esquire, Second Auditor's Office, Treasury Department, Washington."[83] Sedgwick's death was as much a mystery as his birth.

Colonel Sedgwick had served his country with bravery and gallantry. When his country had called for troops, he helped raise a regiment to serve the Union, even though this caused his family ridicule and forced them to leave their home. He had fought with distinction in the Battles of Shiloh, Stone's River and Chickamauga. After President Abraham Lincoln's call for black troops, Sedgwick became a pioneer and helped to raise and command of an African American regiment. Even after the war was over, Colonel Sedgwick remained in command until his country honorably discharged him for his service. Colonel Charles Pennebaker of the 27th Kentucky had this to say of Colonel Sedgwick: "He is a gentleman possessing a high sense of honor, and a gallant soldier, and has rendered valuable services for his country-no man has exhibited more patriotic zeal, and devotion to his country."

Chapter 7

Union Colonel Marcellus Mundy

The leaders of the Civil War were a varied lot. They ranged from experienced to callous, from humble to vainglorious, from strategically brilliant to always a day late and a soldier short. The one thing they had in common was that they cared deeply about how the war was being waged. But Colonel Marcellus Mundy was a rare breed. He was, it seems, more concerned with the general population under his control than with how the war was being fought.[84]

Marcellus Mundy was born on May 16, 1830, at Owen County, Kentucky. He was five feet, ten inches with hazel eyes. While he was only a boy, his father moved to Lexington, Kentucky, in order to educate his sons at the famous Transylvania University. During the 1840s, Marcellus Mundy attended Transylvania University, becoming a member of the Adelphi Society, an early literary organization that promoted artistic interests, libraries and learning. He was also a member of the Whig Society, also known as the Whig-Cliosophic Society, whose principals included education, debate and faultless conduct. The two organizations' goals may have had a strong influence on Mundy's viewpoints about humanity and rights. At the age of sixteen, Mundy graduated with an academic degree. He continued his education by studying law at Transylvania, and after two more years, he graduated with the degree of Bachelor of Arts and Laws.[85]

After graduation, he left Kentucky and traveled to Philadelphia to practice law. At first, he read law for Judge Horton, but he later worked for George Dallas, who was at the time one of the foremost members of the Philadelphia bar. Eventually, Mundy opened a law office of his own.[86]

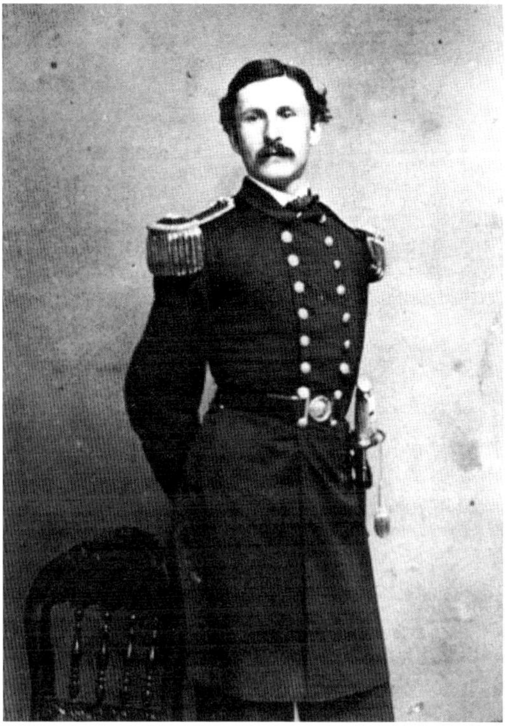

Left: Colonel Marcellus Mundy. *Courtesy of the Old Bardstown Village Inc. Photograph taken by the author.*

Below: Colonel Marcellus Mundy's boxed Schuyler, Hartley and Graham U.S. Regulation chapeau. *Courtesy of the Old Bardstown Village Inc. Photograph taken by the author.*

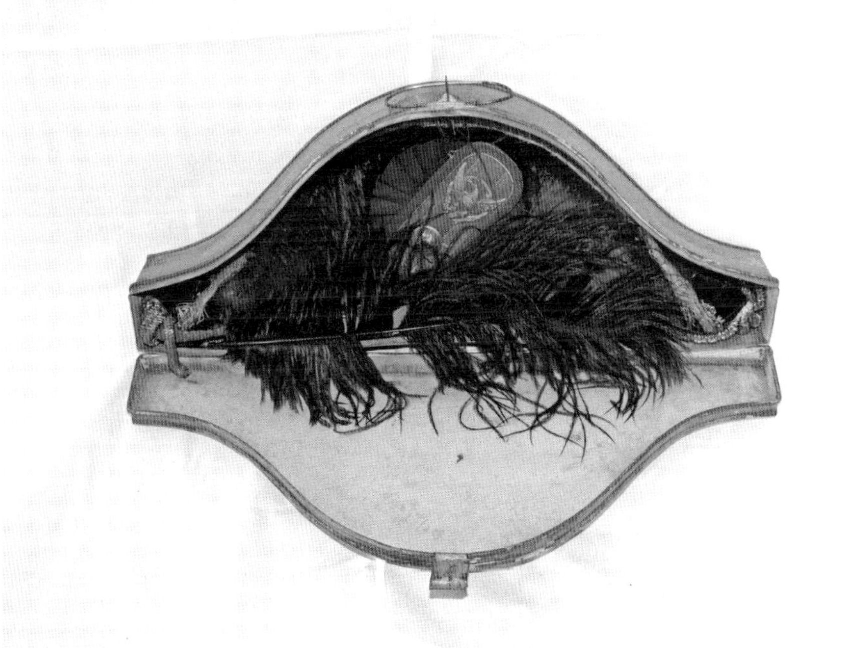

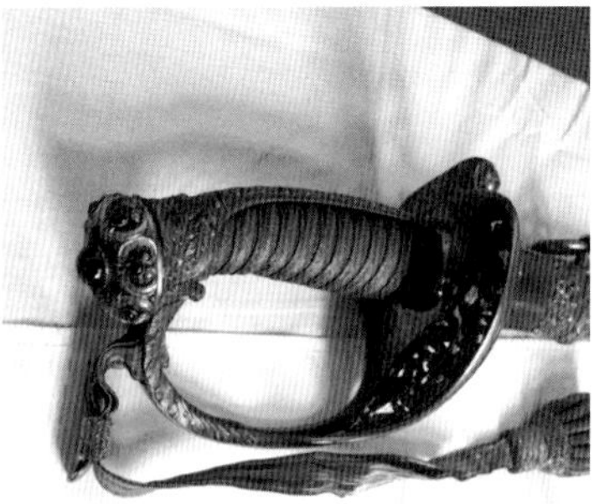

In 1858, he married Margaret Offutt of Scott County, Kentucky, who was but fifteen years old and Mundy's junior by thirteen years. They experienced fewer than three years of martial contentment before the war broke out in April 1861 after the firing on Fort Sumter. A meeting was held by the Philadelphia Bar Association. Many of the bar members made seething speeches against the South, and a motion was made to expel all members who held Southern sentiments. Mundy rose and made a speech asking for all the members for who proposed to fight for the Union to take their position openly and boldly. Mundy offered his services to the Union army and felt that his course of action was much easier than to pass a resolution against certain men who held Southern convictions. Mundy immediately began to recruit men for a regiment.[87]

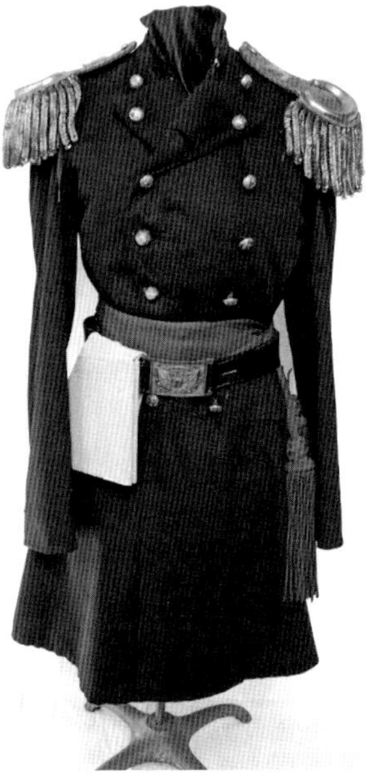

Top: Colonel Marcellus Mundy's Schuyler, Hartley and Graham boxed field officer's sword, inscribed: "Presented to Col. Marc Mundy by the 23rd Ky. Vol. U.S.A. 1862." *Courtesy of the Old Bardstown Village Inc. Photograph taken by the author.*

Middle: Colonel Marcellus Mundy's officer's uniform with Schuyler, Hartley and Graham epaulettes with silver embroidered eagles and Kentucky buttons, along with officer's buffed gloves and officer's sash. *Courtesy of the Old Bardstown Village Inc. Photograph taken by the author.*

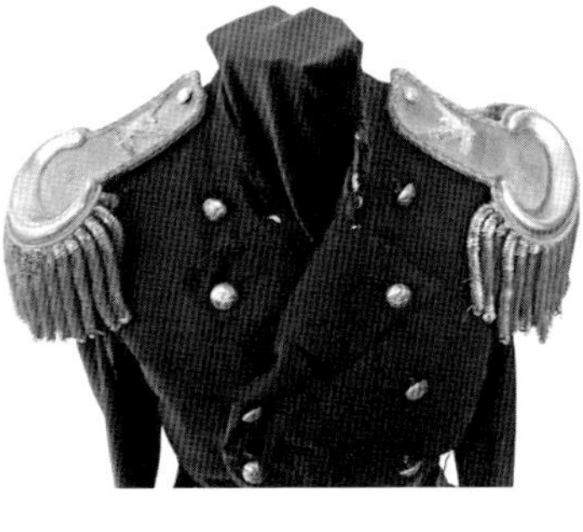

Left: Close-up view of Marcellus Mundy's officer's uniform with epaulettes. *Courtesy of the Old Bardstown Village Inc. Photograph taken by the author.*

Mundy organized the Garibaldi Legion of Philadelphia, and the men elected him colonel of the regiment. He offered his services to the Union government, but since Philadelphia had reached its quota, the legion was not mustered into the Union army. Mundy decided to leave Philadelphia and head for Louisville.[88]

Upon returning to Louisville, Mundy began recruiting and organizing a regiment for the Union army. In September 1861, Mundy, age thirty-one, organized the 23rd Kentucky Infantry at Camp King near Covington, Kentucky. The companies were formed from Mason, Pendleton, Boone, Campbell and Kenton, Kentucky.[89] His brother, William Mundy, who was only seventeen years old at the time, quit Transylvania and joined his brother in the 23rd Kentucky. William was promoted to captain and served as Marc Mundy's adjutant for most of the war.

While at Camp King, the men of the 23rd Kentucky Infantry learned their new trade as soldiers. They remained in camp until February 1862, when the regiment moved to Lexington, followed by Lebanon, Bardstown and, finally, Louisville, Kentucky. Once arriving in Louisville, they boarded the steamer *Diana* and were transported to Nashville, Tennessee. When they arrived, Colonel Mundy, with his regiment and a squadron of cavalry, occupied Lebanon, Tennessee. Colonel Mundy remained in Lebanon for six weeks. He then moved to Murfreesboro, Tennessee, and in May, he took with him to Pulaski, Tennessee, a section of artillery and five hundred cavalrymen.[90]

While in Pulaski, he wrote a letter to President Abraham Lincoln, expressing his concerns over the treatment of the citizens of his home state and the issue of abolishing slavery:

> *The condition of affairs in my native state, Kentucky, alarms and distresses me. I can say, without any exhibition of foolish pride, that our people have displayed the highest patriotism, it patriotism like essential virtue, is to be measured by the resistance of evil temptations. With every affection linked to our Southern brothers to draw us from duty; with unbounded prejudice against the popular abolition sentiment in the north, we aided largely the success of the party on which you are the head, to drive us from duty, and with a strongest disinclination to engage in an unnatural Civil War with our brothers by blood, even for an holy purpose, yet our soldiers fill the ranks of the Union Army, and our citizens while trembling with apprehensions of yet greater evils which may result from a partisan legislation, kneel around the altar of our common country with prayers*

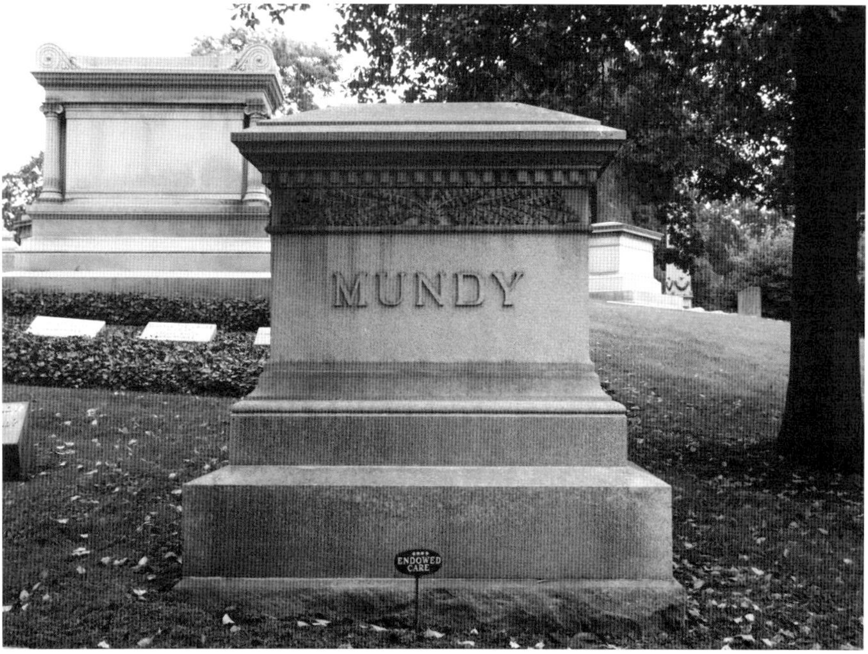

Colonel Marcellus Mundy's family plot, Cave Hill Cemetery. *Photograph taken by the author.*

> *for the preservation of the Federal Constitution and Union, displaying the highest human virtue, resistance to affection's appeals and the persuasions of prejudice.... Opponents to your party in my state, who, forgetting political differences, have formed themselves into a wall of steel around our country's altar to preserve or perish with constitutional liberty, have been outraged by Congressional legislation which libels the cause in which are staked their lives and honor. Kentuckians who have struggled mightily against the claims of affection, who have manfully resisted the prejudice of party and have born meekly vituperative slanders upon their purpose, are eventually being driven from loyalty by the conviction that the Congress of the United States, pursuing partisan fanaticism to the utter disregard of Constitutional right, will abolish slavery.*[91]

Colonel Mundy's sentiment was not unheard of in Kentucky. On the contrary, the sentiment was quite typical. Most Kentuckians were very pro-Union when the war broke out, but Kentucky was also a slaveholding state and traded with both North and South, putting Kentucky in a very unique situation. Colonel Mundy went on to say:

> *Mr. President; they have but little fear but that you will keep good faith with them and the whole country. They have intelligence enough to know that neither you nor the Congress can, constitutionally, abolish slavery in the States....I appeal to you plainly and fairly, as every citizen of the United States has the right to do, and as I have purchased the right to do, by the sacrifice of my domestic comforts, my business, my time, my health, even my life, which has been offered daily for a year, and but awaits the reaper (not for mercenary gain upon contract, as has lately been insinuated in a paper emanating from your Secretary, libeling the whole Volunteer Army), to check unconstitutional legislation which is thus afflicting our people....Mr. President; if in your heart you mean that this conflict shall not degenerate into a war, merely for the abolition of slavery, proclaim this to the world, in undisguised, unambiguous language....Do what is needful now to check disloyal influences and end this war, and boldly write your name where it will be entitled, on the scroll of your country's fame, first beneath that of Washington.*[92]

Although most Kentuckians did not own slaves and full-heartedly supported the Union cause, they still supported the Constitution. Union soldiers in Indiana and other Northern states looked with a suspicious eye on Kentucky because it did not initially join the Union cause and remained neutral. Although Kentucky's legislature was pro-Union, the governor was very supportive of the Confederate cause. This issue would cause Kentucky to become divided. Brother began to fight brother over the issue. Slavery and the Constitution weighed heavily on Colonel Mundy, probably not helping his career, but he felt he had to speak his mind. This would not be the last time; he went on to do so many more times.

In July 1862, Mundy performed court-martial duty at Huntsville, Alabama. In August, he rejoined his command at McMinnville and remained with the 4th Division until it returned to Louisville, Kentucky, in September. While at McMinnville, he found the countryside in poor condition. Food was scarce, "not enough to supply the army by any means." Mundy said that "there was no forage except green corn and hay, and the corn was too green for the use of our stock. We had to rely upon our subsistence department at Murfreesboro for our supplies entirely. My command had only half rations while at McMinnville."[93]

While Mundy was at McMinnville, Union General Don Carlos Buell, commander of the Army of the Ohio, issued General Order No. 13, which basically stated that all loyal citizens were to be treated with consideration

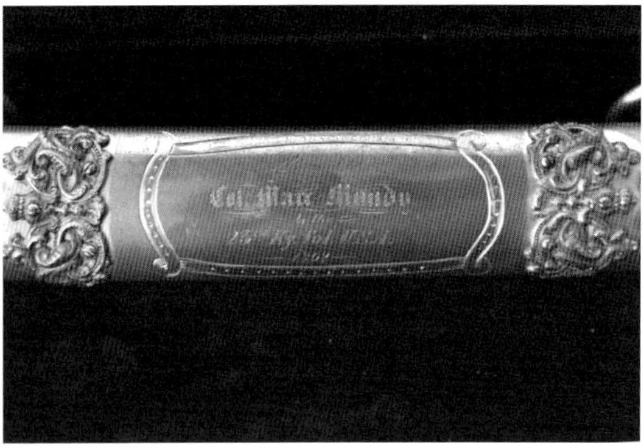

Left: Close-up of Colonel Marcellus Mundy's presentation sword. *Courtesy of the Old Bardstown Village Inc. Photograph taken by the author.*

Below: Close-up of Colonel Marcellus Mundy's presentation sword, sword knot and wooden case made by Schuyler, Hartley and Graham. *Courtesy of the Old Bardstown Village Inc. Photograph taken by the author.*

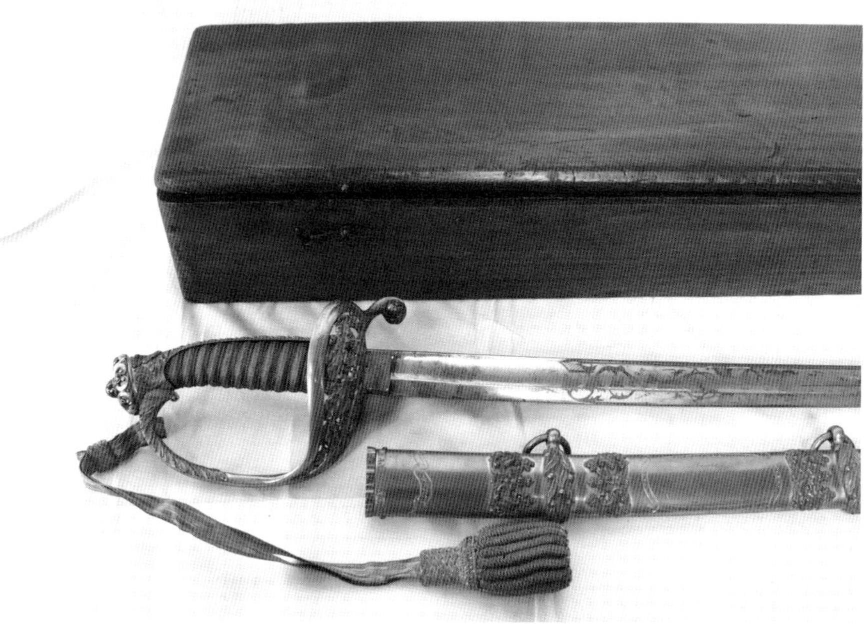

and kindness. Mundy thought that the policy was a just one. He felt that all good citizens in Union-occupied Rebel territory should be protected.[94] He went as far as to remedy some wrongs, protecting them from marauding teamsters and trains that were passing through by issuing an order forbidding depredations on the citizens, forbidding these marauders from taking their property except by his authority.[95]

He had taken a similarly humanistic stance while at Pulaski, where he called a county meeting at the courthouse. Many of the people told him that they favored the restoration of the Union. The people of the town passed a resolution to return to the Union and abandon the Confederacy.

Mundy felt that his policy of showing the people that their property would be protected and their wives and daughters would be safe from ravishing by the hands of the Union army went a long way to gaining their trust and helping them to come back to the Union fold.

Mundy's efforts to protect property rights on both sides even had an effect on Tennessee Governor Andrew Johnson, who formally issued one of Mundy's policies: loyal Union men who had property stolen by Confederate General John Hunt Morgan should be reimbursed for their losses.

To clarify his viewpoint and put weight to his words, Mundy made reference to what happened when loyal citizens were violated. One example was the May 2, 1862 Rape of Athens, when Union Colonel John Basil Turchin unleashed his Union brigade on the undefended town of Athens, Alabama. Turchin, a Russian immigrant known as the "Mad Cossack," let his men loot and pillage the town's stores and homes. "I shut my eyes for two hours. I see nothing," he said before the melee began. At least one girl was raped, and one pregnant woman miscarried and died. The result was that most of the citizens became deeply estranged from the Union cause, and the townspeople lost all confidence in the Union government.[96]

Unfortunately, Mundy's sentiments were not always those of the president and some of the other Union leaders. After the Rape of Athens, Colonel Turchin was court-martialed and found guilty, relieved of command and sent back home to Chicago. But President Lincoln reinstated Colonel Turchin and elevated him to brigadier general, sending a clear signal that the Southern people and property were to be targets for damage. This later became more evident during Union General William T. Sherman's March to the Sea campaign.

On September 1, the 23rd Kentucky arrived in Louisville, Kentucky. On October 1, Mundy was detached to command the military post at Louisville. He would remain in command from October 1 until December 1863. While in command at Louisville, Mundy again became involved in the affairs of the townspeople.

The wives of the Union men who were fighting in the war pleaded with Mundy to help feed their children since there was no income. Mundy wrote to the mayor of Louisville, William Kaye, about the desperate situation:

> *I am overrun with applications from the poor wives and children of soldiers now in the field, serving the government, for assistance to keep them from starving, I deem it my duty to call your attention and that of the city council to the fact. You must consider that the prices of provisions and fuel are much*

enhanced, many of these honest, poor people are forced by pinching necessity to ask for charity. I am now issuing Government rations, without orders, at my personal risk, to many families, who would otherwise starve. And certainly a great city like Louisville could, with little effort, raise a fund for the support of the indigent families of soldiers. I see that Northern cities are appropriating hundreds of thousands of dollars to purchase exemptions and support the poor families of their soldiers, and I respectfully request that the council of the city of Louisville consider the matter.[97]

In March 1863, Colonel Mundy began to experience severe lung problems. It was a preexisting condition that he had for some years. While in Louisville, he was seen by numerous doctors. All the surgeons agreed that Mundy suffered from repeated attacks and hemorrhaged from the lungs, which was a direct result from exposure or fatigue. He was seen as unfit for campaign duty, and it was recommended that he remain in post duty.

That same month, Union General William Rosecrans personally asked for Colonel Mundy to rejoin his command, but Union General Ambrose Burnside, who was at the time the military commander of Kentucky, intervened and informed Rosecrans that Mundy was not well. He was, however, a "very useful officer in Louisville" and should remain there.

Mundy's health continued to decline through that mid-war year, and by December 8, 1863, he could no longer function as a commander. He wrote to Union Major General George Thomas:

[I] *respectfully ask the acceptance of my resignation as Colonel of the 23rd Kentucky Infantry Vols. which I tendered on the 11th day of June last to Maj. General Burnside being physically incapable of doing field duty as will appear from the accompanying surgeons certificate of disability.*

I was ordered from Louisville to summarily when I have been commanding the Post for the last year, that I was compelled to leave all my accounts of the administration of the post fund, some $15,000 and all the accounts of the General Military Administration of the Post Accounting to nearly half a million of dollars to the end of the past current quarter, unsettled and I have to ask respectfully that time and opportunity be allowed me to return to Louisville and adjust all those accounts before the acceptance of my resignation. Let me be permitted to express my regret at being compelled to quit the service before the work…is accomplished but my frail health requires it, and my command having been reduced to about two hundred men by the casualties of war, who have within a full

> *corps of line officers and two field officers of acknowledged bravery and skill, renders my further service unmaterial. If I could be assigned to any duty when my services would be valuable to the government and when I could be shielded from inclement weather I would gladly remain to help our good cause on to success.*
>
> —*Col. Mundy.*[98]

On December 31, 1863, Colonel Mundy's resignation was accepted.

Always mindful of the property rights of others, Mundy's own property became a source of contention after his retirement from military service. A March 8, 1864 letter to Lincoln that is now in the Lincoln Collection at the Library of Congress outlines Mundy's disdain for the property rights handling of the current administration:

> *Mr. President:*
>
> *I had the honor this morning to present your respectful request to the Secretary of War, that he would refer the matter at issue between the government and me regarding the rental of my property at Mound City, Illinois used by the Government for a hospital, to Brig. Gen. Allen, AQM at Louisville, Kentucky for settlement and I regret to inform you that the Hon. Secretary declines to comply with your request. Without detailing the interview I will say to you that I feel compelled to abandon my property as I am satisfied that whatever fair claims I may have as citizen or soldier will be disregarded by the present administration and the urging of them further would but subject me to further discourtesy. I thank you for the courtesy extended to me in our last interview.*
>
> *And have the honor to be*
> *Your obedient servant*
> *M. Mundy.*[99]

A letter to Lincoln the following July 28 makes evident that, while no longer in active service, Mundy kept his hand in political matters. In the letter, he advocates emancipation in Kentucky—if the freed blacks were to be colonized outside Kentucky. Among the reasons Mundy cites for this view is the idea that black people remaining, post-emancipation, within the states' borders would be a source of ongoing enmity in an already divided state,

To our twenty-first-century sensibilities, this might seem racist, "not in my backyard" policy. But if one takes into account the prevailing morals of the times, it can be seen that Mundy's concerns for others is actually at the core of it. It's simply that in this case, his concern was less for the black residents than for his fellow white Kentuckians:

> *Louisville Hotel. Louisville, Ky.*
> *July 28, 1864*
>
> *Mr. President:*
> *Will the Government undertake to Colonize the negroes of Kentucky out of the state, if the people of Kentucky will emancipate them? I do not ask the questions idly, but with the determination to take the stump as an advocate for emancipation if it be answered in the affirmative. Kentucky is the only loyal state in which the institution holds a tenure that cannot be disturbed without manifest wrong and injustice and therefore the more necessity the people should of their own accord dig the root from our soil.*[100]

He goes on to make clear his concern for his fellow Kentuckians and to seek assurances that the government will back a policy that he believes will benefit residents of the state:

> *If Kentucky emancipates, then will slavery in the United States become eradicated, and she certainly will not be asking too much to ask to have them colonized out of her border when emancipated. We need not discuss the causes which may lead the Kentuckians to adopt emancipation as it is sufficient to know that they are ripe for that policy if the government will render a little judicious aid of the kind I suggest. I will give you in brief the suggestions I have made to some of the leading slaver owners of the state: "Our laboring negro men being taken for the army to support the women and children will be a burden and no profit to us as we will in the future have no market south for our slaves. Negroes can never be valuable to us in Ky. when the institution lines our northern and eastern borders."*
>
> *And to those to whom I have conversed upon the subject adopt my views and I can safely say that the only drawback to successful emancipation, is a disinclination to have the negro population freed and kept among us, and certainly the government will, to advance a great scheme like this, fraught with good, forget whatever prejudice may have been engendered against our state by the impolicy of our representative men and to accomplish the great*

work in a lawful and constitutional way, hold our her helping hand. As soon as I receive your affirmative reply I will devote my time and energies to this course.

Respectfully
M. Mundy[101]

Of course, Mundy's hoped-for policies in the postwar years did not come to fruition.

Around the close of the war, Marcellus and his wife, who often went by "Maggie," had a son, whose name in the 1870 census appears to be Marcellus Mundy Jr. Mundy continued to practice law in Louisville. Marc Mundy passed away at his brother William's home on February 22, 1901, from the long illness that had affected his lungs since the Civil War. His final illness came from pneumonia.

His brother, William Mundy, became a prominent Louisville businessman. He originally served in the firm of J.B. Speed as a bookkeeper but was rapidly promoted to a member of the firm. He was a member of the Legion of Honor, whose members were surviving members of the Army of the Cumberland. His son, Offutt Mundy, who was a prominent mechanical engineer, died in Philadelphia. William Mundy never recovered from the death of his son. William Mundy died on December 14, 1906.[102]

Colonel Mundy's legacy was the caring way in which he approached the rights of the citizens, North and South, whose well-being was entrusted to him. It could be said that he saw himself as having two duties: one as a loyal Union officer and another to protect and care for the people under his command. Although Mundy's thinking might have been in opposition to that of some of his Union comrades, Union General Jeremiah T. Boyle said of Mundy, "I believe him as truly loyal as any man in the Army."

Chapter 8

Union General James S. Jackson

On the night of October 7, 1862, Union Generals James S. Jackson, William Terrill and Union Colonel George Webster met on the field at Perryville and discussed their chances of being struck in battle by enemy fire: "Their opinion was that men would never be frightened if they considered the doctrine of probabilities and how slight the chance was on any particular person being killed."[103] On October 8, 1862, the law of probabilities caught up with all three men. This chapter will trace the career and fate of one of those generals: James S. Jackson.

Born in 1823, Kentucky native James Streshly Jackson attended Centre College but left to transfer to Jefferson College in Cannonsburg, Pennsylvania. In 1843, he graduated from Jefferson. Afterward, Jackson became an attorney, practicing in Hopkinsville, Kentucky. During the Mexican-American War, Jackson enlisted and became a third lieutenant in a U.S. volunteer regiment. He resigned his commission when he faced a court-martial for participating in a duel with a fellow officer. On October 11, 1862, the *New York Times* described Jackson as "brusque and overbearing…a party to numerous quarrels, which sometimes resulted in duels."[104] The *Times* also accused Jackson of killing a man in a street fight in Hopkinsville. A quite different impression of Jackson is given on the Kentucky battlefield marker at Perryville, which described him as "impressive in person, graceful in manner, kindly, chivalrous, he was the highest type of Kentucky gentleman."[105]

In the 1860 election, James S. Jackson became a Kentucky Unionist congressman, but when the Civil War broke out in 1861, Jackson left

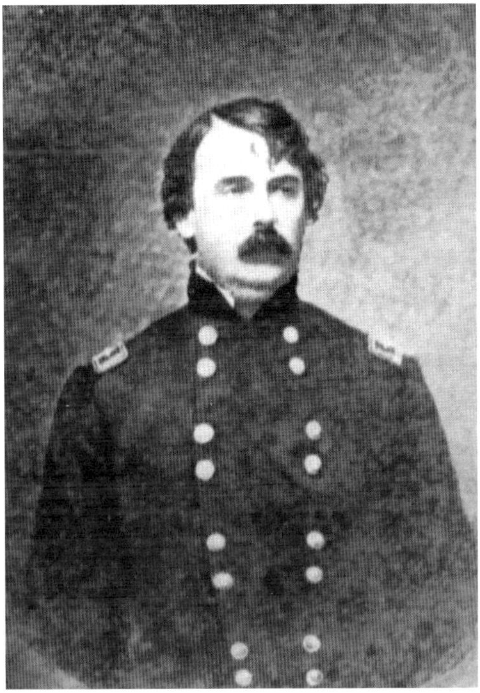

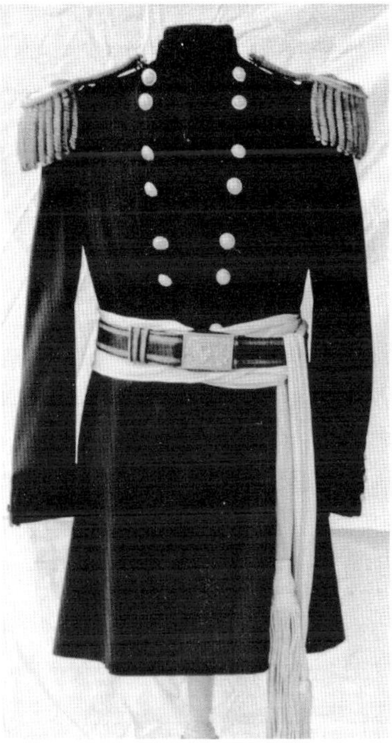

Left: Union General James S. Jackson. *Courtesy of the Old Bardstown Village Inc. Photograph taken by the author.*

Right: Union General James S. Jackson's officer's uniform. *Courtesy of the Old Bardstown Village Inc. Photograph taken by the author.*

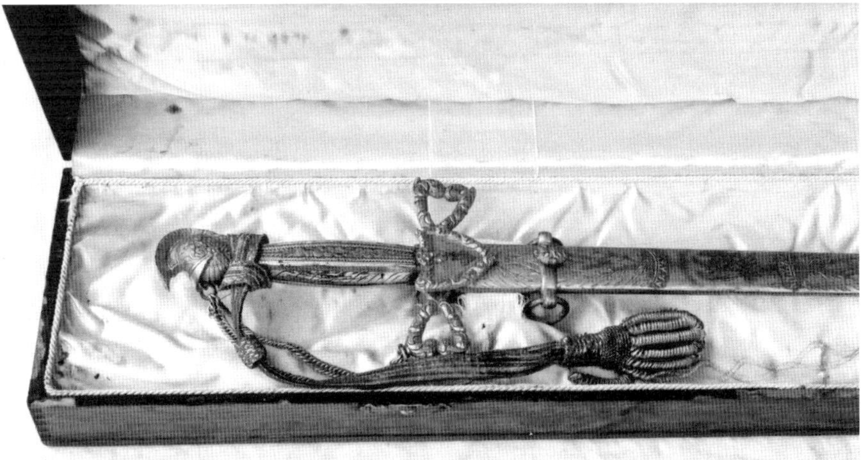

Union General James S. Jackson's boxed presentation grade sword. *Courtesy of the Old Bardstown Village Inc. Photograph taken by the author.*

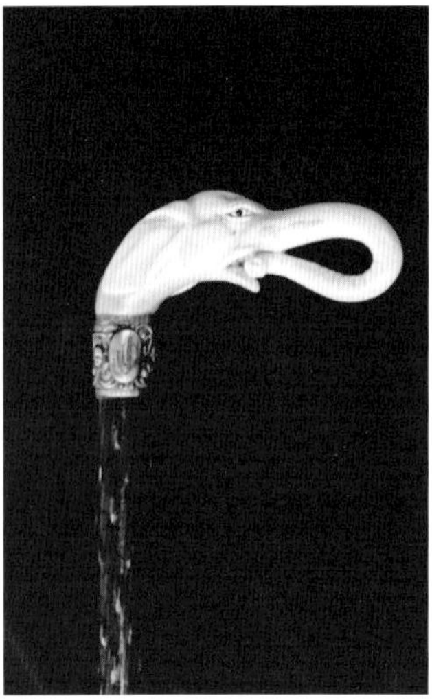

Union General James S. Jackson's ivory-handled walking cane. *Courtesy of the Old Bardstown Village Inc. Photograph taken by the author.*

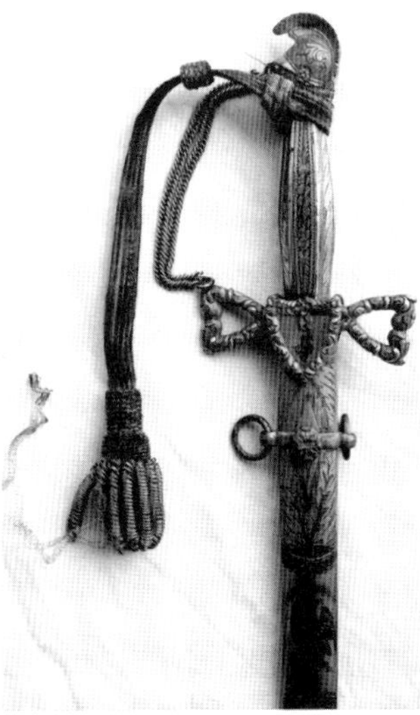

Close-up of Union General James S. Jackson's presentation grade sword. *Courtesy of the Old Bardstown Village Inc. Photograph taken by the author.*

Congress, enlisted in the Union army and became a colonel of the 3rd Kentucky Cavalry on December 13, 1861. After the 3rd Kentucky Cavalry readied itself for service, Colonel Jackson moved out into Tennessee and led his regiment at Shiloh, although his regiment never saw action during the battle. During the advance and siege of Corinth, Mississippi, Jackson took command of all the Union cavalry in the Army of Ohio. Promoted to brigadier general in August 1862, Jackson left for Louisville, Kentucky, to help organize the Union forces gathered to oppose Confederate General Braxton Bragg's Army of Mississippi, which had invaded Kentucky. In September 1862, Jackson became commander of an entire division, composed of the 33rd Brigade, under Brigadier General William Terrill, and the 34th Brigade, under Colonel George Webster.[106]

On October 1, 1862, Union General Don Carlos Buell's Army of the Ohio marched out of Louisville and headed for Bragg's army. Both armies met at Perryville looking for water. On October 6, the Confederates forces under General William Hardee arrived at Perryville first, along with Confederate General Simon Buckner's division. By October 7, Confederate General Patton Anderson and Patrick Cleburne's divisions had arrived at Perryville. On October 7, three Union corps under Alexander McCook, Thomas Crittenden and Charles Gilbert headed for Perryville.[107]

On October 7, General James S. Jackson waited for Union General John Starkweather's brigade to advance, while he marched his division behind Lovell Rousseau's division, with Starkweather's brigade coming on line in the rear. Jackson's division ended up on the Union left. On October 8, 1862, Confederate General Benjamin Cheatham's division advanced on Jackson's position. Confederate General Daniel Donelson's brigade advanced, followed by Confederate General Alexander Stewart's command. As Donelson's men approached Colonel Terrill's brigade, he came upon the eleven guns of Colonel Charles Parson's battery. General Stewart's brigade also came under the fire of Parson's battery. Cheatham ordered the brigade of General George Maney to take the battery and encircle the Union left.

Sheltered from view by the wooded hills, Maney's men emerged into view of Jackson's men. Union General James Jackson was with Colonel Parson's battery when Maney's brigade approached to within three hundred yards of his men. Jackson ordered the battery to redirect its fire to face the new threat. Eight cannons fired canister shot into Maney's ranks. The 123rd Illinois, General Terrill's brigade, opened fire on Maney's men. Maney's men cleared a picket fence and charged into Jackson's men. A hail of bullets from Maney's soldiers rained down on Jackson's men, intensifying as Maney's men got closer to Jackson's position. Jackson remarked, "Well, I'll be damned if this is not getting rather particular." As soon as Jackson spoke, a Confederate bullet immediately struck Jackson in the chest. Union Captain Samuel Starling stated that the bullet killed Jackson instantly, but Union Captain Percival Oldershaw witnessed Jackson fall to the ground and said that he found Jackson "on his back, struggling to speak, but unable to do so. He died in a few moments." Oldershaw stated that two bullets entered Jackson's chest.[108]

After Jackson was killed, the 123rd Illinois panicked and fell back. Maney continued his assault and overwhelmed the Union line under Jackson. Parson's battery lost half its men and officers, and the battery fell into Confederate hands, except for one gun. The Union line fell back to the Benton road on the next hill to the rear. The Confederates moved toward Starkweather's hill, where Bush's and Stone's battery faced the oncoming Confederates. During the battle, General Terrill was killed by an artillery shell. The Federal line held at Starkweather's hill. General Cheatham's line fell back beyond the ridge from where it had originally driven the Union line. The battle for the Union left was over.[109] Union General James Jackson, William Terrill and Colonel George Webster all became fatalities.

After the battle, Union General James Jackson was buried at Cave Hill Cemetery in Louisville, Kentucky, but later reinterred in Hopkinsville, Kentucky. The Kentucky Historical Society erected a marker to James Jackson that stands at the site of his death at Perryville, Kentucky.

Little did James S. Jackson, William Terrill and George Webster know that on a bloody, hot fall day in 1862 the law of averages would catch up with all three of them—all sacrificed their lives for the Union, but the losses of these three officers were not in vain. Although the Union army, under General Don Carlos Buell, suffered heavy losses and lost the battle on October 8, 1862, Confederate General Braxton Bragg did not renew the battle the next day. He pulled his army out of Perryville and headed for Tennessee, leaving Kentucky in Union hands for the rest of the war.

Chapter 9

Union Lieutenant Colonel Charles Gill

Charles Gill was educated at the University of Louisville and was an excellent scholar. When the Civil War erupted on the American landscape in April 1861, Gill made three unsuccessful attempts to join the Union army while in school, but the Union enlistment agents denied him because of his youth. In July 1862, the Union army finally accepted Gill, and he joined the 2nd Kentucky Cavalry. Colonel Buckner Board formed the cavalry regiment at Camp Joseph Holt near Jeffersonville, Indiana, under Union General Lovell Rousseau's brigade.[110]

In September 1861, the regiment moved out of Camp Joe Holt, crossed into Louisville and marched along the Louisville and Nashville Railroad, with orders to engage Confederate General Simon Buckner's Confederate forces. While at Camp Nevin, Private Gill was detached to a mounted cavalry to General Alexander McDowell McCook. Shortly afterward, he was in his first fight, at Woodsonville, Kentucky, also known as the Battle of Rowlett's Station, Kentucky, under Colonel August Willich's command, with the Confederate forces under Colonel Benjamin Franklin Terry.[111]

After the Battle of Rowlett's Station, Gill was involved in the Battle of Shiloh on April 6 and 7 of 1862. He was with General McCook when, seeing an officer's horse shot out under him, he offered him his own horse. Since Gill no longer had a horse, he grabbed a musket and cartridge box from a dead soldier and fought with an Indiana regiment for the rest of the day.

He received an injury to his hip in fording the Rolling Fork River when his regiment marched from Lebanon Junction, Kentucky—the exposure from the heavy rain at Shiloh caused an inflammation and forced him to be removed to a hospital, where he lay up for several months, using crutches for several weeks afterward and slightly lame from the injury.

On his way back to his regiment after his recovery from his injury, he was detained at Nashville, Tennessee, and placed on duty, with the Rebel forces being near the city. Shortly after duty at Nashville, Generals Alexander McCook, Lovell Rousseau and James Negley recommended that Gill be promoted. In December 1863, Gill was promoted to second lieutenant of the 5th Kentucky Cavalry.

Gill participated in the Siege of Corinth, Mississippi; the Battle of Resaca, Georgia; the Battle of Atlanta; and the Battle of Jonesboro, acting as aide de camp to General Hugh Judson Kilpatrick in his sixteen-day raid around the Confederate army when, at Lovejoy Station, they were surrounded by three divisions of infantry and cavalry. The cavalry had to literally cut its way out with their sabers.

At Campbelltown, in the fall of 1864, Lieutenant Gill, with part of his company, recaptured General Kilpatrick's wagon train, receiving the general's thanks and recommendation for promotion.

Gill traveled along during Union General William T. Sherman's March to the Sea campaign. At Waynesboro, the captain of Gill's company was killed at his side. From this time forward, Gill had charge of the company. At a bridge across the Altamaha River, Gill was struck with a spent ball.

On March 16, 1864, Gill was promoted to first lieutenant of Company K, 5th Kentucky Cavalry. In February 1865, he was promoted to adjutant, and on May 5, 1865, he was promoted to major of the 5th Kentucky Cavalry; on the same day, he was brevetted lieutenant colonel for "gallant and meritorious conduct in battle." On August 9, 1865, Gill was mustered out.

After the war, Gill returned to Louisville, studied law and was admitted to the bar. He became a prominent attorney in Louisville and was elected prosecuting attorney for the city court, a position he held until his death. His funeral was held at the Walnut Street Baptist Church, and all the well-known men in Louisville and the city officials attended his funeral. After the funeral, a few of his friends followed his body to Cave Hill Cemetery.[112]

Chapter 10

Union General William Howard Irwin

William Howard Irwin was born on January 17, 1818, in Mifflin County, Pennsylvania. In 1836, he joined Dickinson College in Carlisle, Pennsylvania, and enrolled with the class of 1840. He was a member of the Union Philosophical Society, but after two years, he left the college to study law at home in Lewistown. In 1842, he became a member of the bar. In 1843, he married Edmiston Mitchell.

He continued to practice law in Lewistown until 1847, when he traveled to Washington, D.C., to request a commission in the 11th U.S. Infantry. He returned to Lewistown to recruit an infantry unit from Mifflin County for service in the Mexican-American War. His company became known as the Juanita Guards, Company D, 11th U.S. Infantry. On March 25, 1847, the Juanita Guards left Lewistown. On September 8, 1847, with the 11th U.S. Infantry serving under Gideon Pillow's Division, Irwin's company fought at the Battle of El Molino del Rey, where Irwin was seriously wounded while at the head of his company. In August 1848, following his recuperation, Irwin was brevetted a major for his bravery during the battle and returned home to Lewistown.

Irwin returned to his law practice in Lewistown until Confederate forces fired on Union-held Fort Sumter on April 12, 1861. Irwin heeded the call for volunteers and joined as a private serving in the Logan Guards. The Logan Guards, along with Irwin, helped to secure the national capital from sudden attack. The Federal government transferred him from the Logan Guards to the 7th Pennsylvania Volunteer Infantry and commissioned him as colonel. During their ninety-day enlistment, the 7th Pennsylvania participated in the early movement on the Shenandoah Valley during the summer of 1861. When the 7th Pennsylvania Infantry was mustered out, Irwin assisted in the recruitment and organizing of Pennsylvania regiments until he was appointed colonel of the 49th Pennsylvania Volunteer Infantry in late 1861.

During the training of the 49th Pennsylvania, Irwin was involved in a controversy when several officers under his command filed charges and he was tried under court-martial early in 1862 for drunkenness and "conduct prejudicial to good order and military discipline." Irwin was acquitted on the first charge but convicted on the second charge. The military tribunal gave Irwin an inconsequential punishment, and he went on to command his regiment.

During the Battle of Williamsburg, Virginia, Irwin and the 49th Pennsylvania formed in line of battle on the left of the 1st Brigade and moved forward in support of a battery on the right in the open ground in front of the second fort, over which the Confederate colors were hoisted. The men were ordered to lie down during the rapid and heavy artillery fire and remained until Lieutenant Mitchell of the brigade staff informed Colonel Irwin that the Rebels had moved in force from the woods on their right and poured a severe fire into their ranks. Irwin formed his line, and seeing the battery retiring and the 6th Maine Infantry and the other regiments on his right returning to their original line on the flanks of the fort, Irwin faced by the rear rank and marched at the parade step, faced front and began to fire on the Confederate forces, who were rapidly and boldly advancing and were in good rifle range. Irwin ordered his right wing to fire obliquely to the right, and their close and steady volley struck with terrible effect on the Rebel forces. When they came within easy range, the whole line opened fire on the Confederate infantry.

When Union General Winfield Hancock ordered the line forward to charge, the Rebels who were rushing upon Irwin's forces, with his regiment loudly cheering, moved rapidly and steadily to the front, with their colors advanced and their line accurate. A Confederate regiment advanced to the woods on Irwin's left. Irwin deployed by the left flank two of his companies (both I and K) as skirmishers, covered the left of the line and held the woods until the Confederates retreated. As far as possible, all random firing was prevented. Irwin ordered his men to fire low and select their marks carefully. Irwin praised his men in his official report. His men were weary, had lost sleep, made a forced march over bad roads in horrible

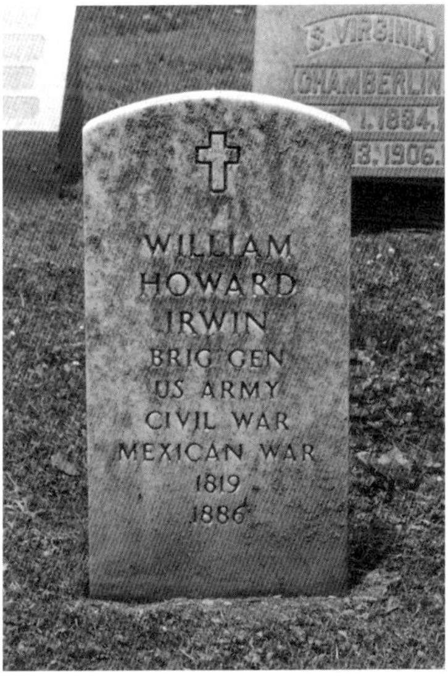

General William Howard Irwin's tombstone, Cave Hill Cemetery. *Photograph taken by the author.*

weather and were confronting the Rebels for the first time, but they held their ground during the battle as if they were veterans.[113] After the battle, General Hancock, commanding the 1st Brigade, gave the highest commendations to Colonel William Irwin for his actions during the battle.

During the Seven Days Battles on the Peninsular Campaign on June 28, 1862, Colonel Irwin ordered Companies D and I and part of Company A, in all one hundred men, to proceed to the picket line and relieve the 77th New York Infantry. Captain James Campbell of the 49th Pennsylvania found the 77th New York in front of the dam on Garrett's Farm. Campbell posted one-third of his force on the line on the brow of the hill, the left resting at the earthwork; the remaining force was placed under cover in the edge of a timber line, near the angle, in support. At about 11:00 a.m., the Confederate artillery opened fire and continued to fire for about half an hour, when Irwin observed two Rebel infantry regiments approach in line of battle, a heavy column closed in mass in the rear marching toward the right, where Captain Miles was posted. Campbell ordered his men to open fire. The Rebels halted and laid down; those who were marching to the right had already made the timber line.

Campbell moved the support from the angle of the woods about fifty yards to the right in order to leave the front commanded by the rifle pits open and to be out of the range of the artillery. The Rebels advanced, returning the fire of the 49th Pennsylvania pickets, who were compelled to retire before being outnumbered, but not until they succeeded in driving in the Confederate skirmishers and following the 2nd Division of their corps. The brigade reached Banks Ford and crossed the river. The 49th Pennsylvania camped near Berea Church and remained with the rest of the 6th Corps to cover the return of the pontoons. Colonel Irwin was seriously wounded on June 28, 1862, when crossing the river.[114]

By September 1862, Irwin was commanding the 3rd Brigade, which comprised the 7th Maine Infantry under Major Thomas Hyde, the

20th New York under the command of Colonel Ernest von Vegesack, the 33rd New York under the command of Lieutenant Colonel Joseph Coming, the 49th New York under Lieutenant Colonel William Alberger and the 77th New York under Captain Nathan Babcock. On September 14, a division order sent Irwin's brigade to support General William Brooks, who was already engaging the Rebels at Crampton's Pass. The battle moved rapidly and steadily through Burkittsville. The shells thrown at Brooks's flank from the battery south of the pass did no injury. Irwin reached the crest of the mountain after dark; finding that the Confederates had broken and that General Brooks had marched in pursuit into the valley, Irwin reported to Brooks just beyond the pass and, by his order, established the 7th Maine, 20th New York, 33rd New York and 77th New York close in the rear of Captain Romeyn Ayres's battery, sending forward the 49th New York as skirmishers by the road leading to the Catoctin Mountain.[115]

On September 17, Irwin moved with the division toward Sharpsburg, near which very heavy and continuous firing was heard; at about 10:00 a.m., Irwin formed on the field of battle near Antietam Creek, on the left of the 1st Brigade, and was immediately ordered into action by Major General William "Baldy" Smith. Two of the regiments, the 33rd and 77th New York, were sent as skirmishers on the right; the 7th Maine and the 49th and 20th New York were kept in line of battle. The brigade, animated by the words of General Smith and by their own officers, dashed at the Confederates in high spirits and good order and was soon hotly engaged by the Rebels, but the men could not endure the brigade's charge and broke in confusion.

A severe and unexpected volley from the woods on Irwin's right struck full on the 77th and 33rd New York, staggering them for a moment, but they closed up and faced by the rear rank, pouring in a close and scorching fire and driving back and scattering the Confederates. As soon as Irwin's line was formed, facing the belt of the woods and the open ground to the right, the men were ordered down. Pickets were posted on the crest of a small hill along their front, and all were kept in readiness to hold firmly to the position or to attack. A Confederate battery advanced and played with severity along Irwin's flank and through the line of the 20th New York, which, from the nature of the ground, was compelled to refuse its left and received the fire along its entire front. Sharpshooters from the woods to the right and the extreme left also opened up on Irwin's brigade. Shell, grape and canister swept from left to right. The Confederate battery kept up an accurate and rapid fire, and in a short time, Irwin's losses began to take a huge toll in dead and wounded.

At 4:00 p.m., Captain Emory Upton, chief of artillery of General Henry Slocum's division, rode to Irwin's line, and after they examined the ground in front of their left, Irwin decided to accept the battery that Upton earnestly advised him to have planted there. The Confederates were massing in front with the purpose of throwing a column against Irwin's left, and they could not be seen except from that part of the line. Irwin sent word to Major General Smith, who approved the movement, and he requested Captain Upton to order up his battery, which came into action very quickly and opened fire with three rifled cannons; after firing on the Rebels with great effect for half an hour, they were withdrawn and replaced by a battery of Napoleon cannons, whose fire was terribly destructive. The Napoleons were of great value to Irwin and his men.

When the battery was fully engaged, there was a group of sharpshooters on the skirt of the woods on Irwin's left and front. For the protection of the battery, Irwin found that he had to dislodge them. The 7th Maine, under Major Thomas Hyde, was sent forward to his men to eliminate the sharpshooter threat. The regiment advanced in front of the skirmishers of the brigade on the left. The major threw out skirmishers, who soon drove the Rebels from the edge of the cornfield and the hollow lying on the side of the woods. The battalion was ordered forward, and as the Confederates opened fire on the woods from the front and left flank, a charge was ordered; with fixed bayonets, the men pushed forward in line with a cheer, advancing nearly a quarter mile at the double quick. Being outflanked, the Confederates in the orchard to the left broke and ran. The Rebels who were directly in the front behind haystacks and outbuildings also broke and ran; their flags having fallen, the 7th Maine pushed on up the hill to secure the flags when a Confederate regiment suddenly rose from behind a stone wall on its right, pouring a volley. At the same time, the men double-quicked around to the left to cut off the retreat. Seeing the small numbers of Confederates, those in front rallied, and the Rebels advanced in force. Four of their Rebel flags were seen, and battery opened fire on the 7th Maine with grape—they were partly shielded from this, however, by the trees in the orchard.

Finding the regiment engaged, Irwin was very anxious to support the men, but his orders were specific, stating that he could not advance his line. Irwin rode rapidly forward and requested the officer commanding the right regiment of the 2nd Brigade to support Major Hyde, which he declined to do without orders from General Brooks. Irwin returned to his own line to ask for a support from the rear, but in a few minutes, he had the pleasure of seeing the shattered but brave remnant of the 7th Maine return in good order to Irwin's lines. Alone and surrounded by the Confederates, the 7th Maine fought until nearly all cartridges were spent. The men then delivered one fierce parting volley, closed their ranks around their colors and fell slowly back to the line of battle.

The 20th New York was exposed to the heaviest fire. Colonel Von Vegesack was under fire with his men constantly, and his calm and courage was example to his men. Their flag was riddled with balls and shells, and their killed and wounded amounted to 145 men.

The 49th New York, led by Colonel W.C. Alberger, charged with the brigade in the morning on September 17 and drove the Confederates before them, taking their place in line of battle, which they held firmly until they were relieved on September 18. Colonel Alberger was severely wounded in the face by a splinter of shell. The 77th New York and 33rd New York on Irwin's right, under Captain N.S. Babock and Lieutenant Colonel Joseph Corning, repulsed the Confederates and then took and held firmly their place in line of battle until they were relieved.

Lieutenant Martin, 5th Artillery, part of the command of Captain Ayres, which was posted near Irwin's right, engaged the Confederates for several hours at short range with deadly effect. Irwin complimented the battery, stating that Ayres battery helped keep his brigade safe. Ayres checked the heavy Confederate battery fire and prevented them from destroying a greater part of Irwin's command.

At 10:00 a.m., the brigade charged the Confederates and drove them from their ground, which had been hotly contested; it occupied and held the ground for twenty-six hours until it was relieved at noon the next day by General Darius Couch's division. Irwin's brigade was under constant fire during this time in an exposed position and lost 311 killed and wounded, yet neither officers nor men fell back. Irwin's line was "immovable, only anxious to be launched against the enemy."

On April 29, 1863, at the Battle of Fredericksburg, while crossing the river in the pontoons under fire, Irwin was wounded in the foot. By October 1863, Irwin was plagued by illness and wounds. Suffering from mental exhaustion, he was declared unfit for field service, and he resigned his commission.

After the war, Irwin was brevetted a brigadier general for his service and his conduct at Antietam. After the death of his first wife, in 1876 he married Julia Cynthia Chamberlain, who was reported to be the reigning belle of Louisville and was much younger than Irwin. He had one son by her. He returned to his law practice in Louisville, Kentucky, and was twice a candidate for Congress. He was even mentioned for the governorship, but Irwin failed in politics "because he was more of a student than a politician."[116] He was also a scientist of some ability. He also was involved in railroads and mining, but business affairs "did not favor him with fortune."[117] Unfortunately, on October 14, 1885, Irwin was committed to Anchorage Insane Asylum. He had been deemed hopelessly insane by doctors. At times, he tried to kill his wife and son. During his lucid moments, he would beg his wife to have him confined. General Irwin passed away on January 17, 1886, in the Anchorage Insane Asylum at the age of sixty-five.

Chapter 11

Confederate Colonel Philip Lee

Philip Lee was born on October 22, 1832, in Bullitt County. His father, Wilford Lee, migrated from Virginia early in life and was related to the famous Lees of Virginia. At the age of eighteen, Philip graduated from St. Joseph's College in Bardstown, Kentucky. In 1852, at the age of twenty, he graduated from the University of Louisville and was admitted to the bar. He practiced law in Bullitt County, Kentucky, and the surrounding counties. In 1853, he was elected to represent Bullitt County in the Kentucky legislature, and in 1855, he was reelected.[118]

In 1856, he was a candidate for the presidential elector on the Millard Fillmore and Andrew Donelson ticket, in opposition to the Beriah Magoffin on the ticket for James Buchanan and John C. Breckinridge. In 1860, he was a elector on the John Bell and Everett ticket for the Constitutional Unionist Party, opposed by Captain E.A. Graves on the Democratic Stephen Douglas ticket and M.R. Hardin on the ticket for the Southern Democratic John Breckinridge and Lane ticket. While canvassing for the candidates, he became known as a popular debater.[119]

In 1861, the Civil War broke out across the country when Confederate forces fired on Fort Sumter in the Charleston, South Carolina harbor. The Kentucky legislature decided to take a stance of neutrality and stayed out of the conflict. Lee spoke out against neutrality and tried to convince the legislatures to side with the Confederacy. Lee decided to recruit men for the Confederate service, breaking Kentucky's neutrality.

He took his recruits to a point on the Tennessee border with Kentucky. On July 4, 1861, with Confederate Generals Lloyd Tilghman and John Breckinridge, he assisted in the layout of Camp Boone. On July 16, 1861, he was elected Captain of Company C, 2nd Kentucky Infantry, 1st Brigade of Infantry. Commander Colonel Bob Johnson of the 2nd Kentucky ordered Lee to take command of one hundred men and cross into Kentucky, with the purpose of disarming the Home Guard and securing arms of the Confederate troops at Camp Boone.[120]

On August 20, Lee marched out with his men, captured a train of cars and came close to Bowling Green, Kentucky, but the alarm had been raised through telegraph and newspapers of his impending approach. The route was abandoned by the local militia. Lee returned to Camp Boone with no arms for the Confederate forces.[121]

At the Battle of Fort Donelson in February 1862, Lee, along with most of the Confederate forces, were surrendered to Union General Ulysses S. Grant's forces. Lee was held in captivity for six months. Once he was released, he fought in every engagement in which his regiment was engaged during the war, except for July 22 near Atlanta, Georgia. At the Battle of Chickamauga in September 1863, Lee was sick and was acting field officer but fought with gallantry. Shortly after the battle, he was promoted to major, and on November 5, he was promoted to lieutenant colonel.[122]

On the campaign from Dalton, Georgia, to Atlanta, Lee received a painful wound at the Battle of Resaca on May 14, and on May 28, at the Battle of Dallas, he was wounded again. After the fall of Moss at Jonesboro on August 31, 1864, Lee was promoted to colonel and commanded the 2nd Kentucky until 1865. Toward the end of the war, at McClernand's Ford in South Carolina, Lee, along with his regiment, succeeded in repulsing and heading off an overwhelming Federal force, saving the brigade train from falling into Union hands.[123]

After the war, Lee resumed his practice in Bardstown as a lawyer and formed a partnership with Colonel W.R. Grigsby, becoming one of the leading attorneys. On June 23, 1866, he married Bell Bridgeford. Her father, James Bridgeford, was one of the leading stove manufacturers in the country. In December 1866, many of Lee's friends suggested that he be nominated for the position of lieutenant governor. In 1867, he moved to Louisville, Kentucky, and formed a partnership with D.M. Rodman.[124]

At the Democratic convention held in Louisville on May 1868, Lee was nominated for the position of commonwealth attorney of the Ninth

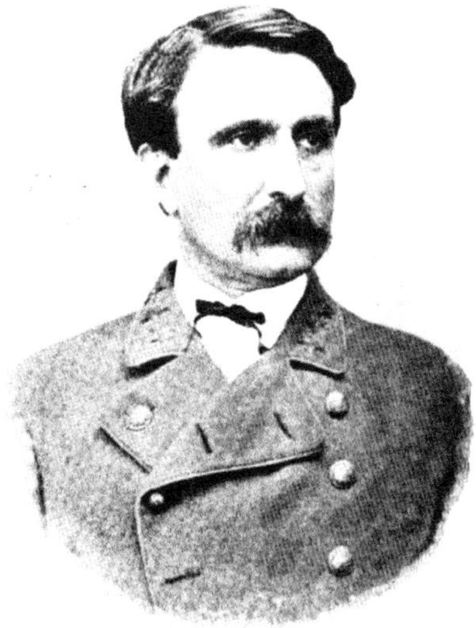

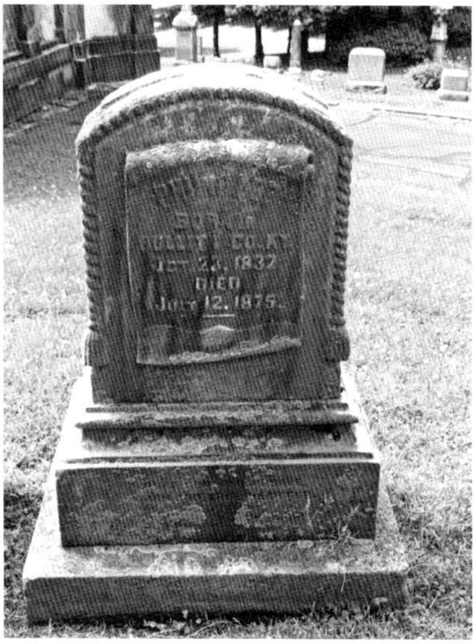

Left: Confederate Colonel Philip Lee. *From Ed Porter Thompson's* History of the First Kentucky Brigade *(Caxton Publishing, 1868).*

Right: Colonel Philip Lee's tombstone, Cave Hill Cemetery. *Photograph taken by the author.*

Judicial District and won the election. He began his term in office in September 1868 and mastered the law and practice in criminal trials, becoming one of the best commonwealth attorneys in the country. He made murder unpopular in Louisville. He was reelected in 1874. He died on July 12, 1875. When news was announced of his death, bells began to toll on Louisville, and the city flags were lowered to half-staff. His funeral was held at Cavalry Church, and he was laid to rest at Cave Hill Cemetery.[125]

On July 13, 1875, the *Louisville Commercial* newspaper published the following tribute to Colonel Lee:

> *He filled the position of prosecuting attorney with distinguished ability. As a pleader the Louisville bar has had but few men who could compare to Col. Lee. Brilliant and passionate as a speaker, he never failed to exert a wonderful effect upon the jury; and for the first time in the history of the court, a distinguished attorney for the defense in a certain case based a motion for a new trial on the ground of the undue influence of Col. Lee's passionate eloquence upon the jury. He was the most*

severe prosecutor that the Circuit Court has ever had, and perhaps did more to enforce the law and mete out justice to criminals than any man who ever held the position. It is said that while he was prosecuting there was not a single verdict of acquittal on the charge of homicide.[126]

Chapter 12

Confederate General Thomas Harris

Thomas Harris was born in the Virginia valley near Winchester in May 1826. He traveled with his father to Missouri when he was a boy and lived near Hannibal. At the age of nine, he was orphaned and clerked in various stores near Hannibal in order to survive. As a young boy, he had an innate love for the military and studied tactics and military government. In 1838, at the age of twelve, he was placed in command of militia unit and sent out after Joseph Smith and his Mormon followers. He was largely instrumental in ridding the state of Missouri of the Mormons. He also fought in the Iowa War and was elected lieutenant colonel of a militia regiment at the age of seventeen.[127]

In 1843, he attended the United States Military Academy at West Point, where he was friends with Ulysses S. Grant and Simeon Buckner. He did not graduate from West Point and left in 1845. He studied law, but he could not stay away from the military. In 1848, he was commissioned a lieutenant in the 12th U.S. Infantry, but peace was declared to end the Mexican-American War. In early 1850, he was given command of troops sent from Missouri and participated in the Lopez filibustering expedition to Cuba. As colonel, Harris led another filibustering expedition into Central America. Returning to Hannibal in the 1850s, Harris became the legal counsel for the local railroad and served as city attorney. He also edited a local newspaper.[128]

He married the sister of Admiral Alexander Porter of the United States Navy. He made an extended tour of Europe with his wife and resided in London, Paris and Vienna. His wife died shortly after he returned to

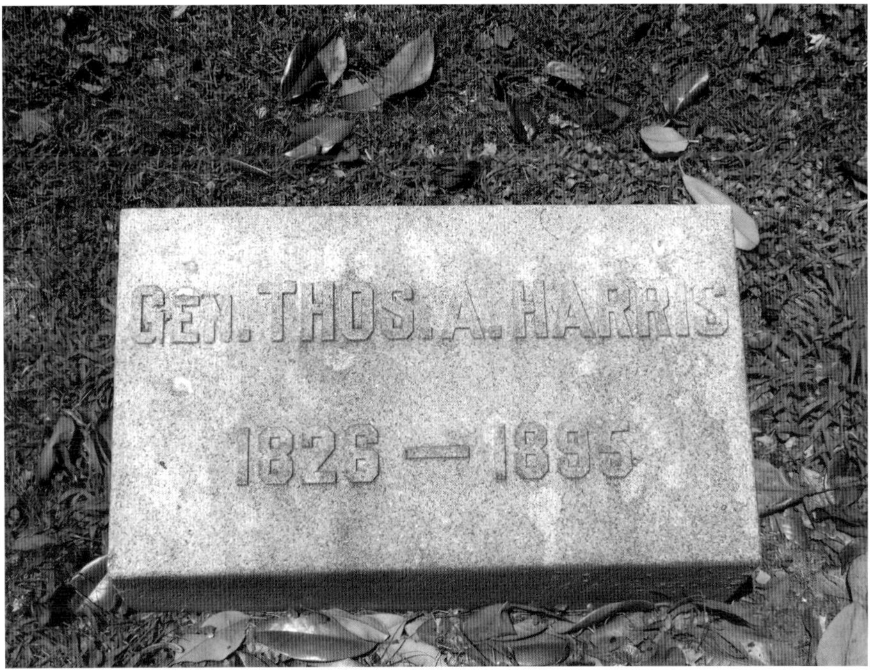

General Thomas Harris's grave, Cave Hill Cemetery. *Photograph taken by the author.*

Missouri. He was then sent to the Missouri legislature. He was the only man in Missouri who was selected to appear against Thomas Hart Benton in a joint debate. Benton had served thirty-five years in the Senate and was the only member to serve five terms. He was known as "Old Bullion Benton." He was an imperious man who would not brook contradiction. He was also a staunch advocate and architect of westward expansion, which became known as Manifest Destiny.

Harris liked to tell the story of his debate with Benton. Benton spoke first and Harris followed. Harris's speech was mostly a parody of Benton's bombastic style. Benton looked and listened in amazement. His amazement soon turned to anger. Finally, Harris's portrayal of him so angered Benton that he left the stage in a high state of indignation and disgust. Harris apologized to Benton, who became friendly. Benton was defeated, and much credit is given by Harris for the defeat.[129]

Harris went to Mexico, where he received commercial concessions from the Mexican government. He organized the Mexican Trade and Transportation Company, which included the establishment of railroad and steamship communication with the United States. The scheme fell through due to lack of capital. Harris was a resident of Mexico City for a number of years.[130]

In 1856, Harris made an unsuccessful run for secretary of state in Missouri on the anti-Benton ticket. In 1860, he was elected to the state House of Representatives on the Bell-Everett ticket. He was also chosen as chairman of the House military committee.[131]

When the Civil War broke out, part of the Missouri State Guard took sides with the Confederacy, and General Sterling Price was given command. While traveling to Booneville to join Governor Claiborne Jackson, Harris received a message on June 21, 1861, informing him that the governor had commissioned him a brigadier general of the 2nd Division of the Missouri State Guard. After receiving his commission, Harris managed to raise more than two thousand men in northwest Missouri.[132]

On September 18, 1861, Harris marched with his division toward Lexington, Missouri, to take on Union Colonel James Mulligan's 3,500 men, who controlled Lexington. His whole command acted as infantry and moved by the flank, with the battery of artillery bringing up the rear. Harris had proceeded about one mile when his advance troops came upon Confederate General Mosby Parson's division, and he soon after received orders to take the road to the left and support the movements of Parson's division. An order to bring Harris's artillery to the advance caused the delay of some fifteen minutes, as the infantry had to move out of the way for the passage of Parson's division along the road. Harris's command arrived at 10:00 a.m., and he ordered Captain James Kneisley, who was in command of the battery, to take position at an elevated point of intersection of two streets, open fire and imitate the movements of the battery of General Parson's division, which was already in action. He detached Captain Davis's company, armed with rifled muskets, to act as an intermediate covering party for the battery, while his whole command, protected by houses, was held in readiness to support the battery if required. Captain Kneisley's battery fire was destructive on the Union forces. At one or two positions occupied by Harris's command, the Union forces fired grape and round shot, but a slight change in position helped to protect his forces against artillery fire.[133]

At 11:00 a.m., Harris received an order from Confederate General Sterling Price to move his command along the bank of the river to support Confederate General James McBride's command and Confederate General William Slack's division, under the command of Colonel Ben Rives. At the same time, Price gave Harris instructions to capture the Anderson house, which was located outside the Union's line of defense, provided that Harris could hold the position at the house without a severe loss. Harris's battery remained in its position.

Harris moved his command along to the line of the river, ordering his men to crawl to the crests of the hills and annoy the Federals as they exposed themselves above their breastworks. Lieutenant Colonel Brace's battalion held to occupy the main road for several hours as a reserve.

When Harris reached the Anderson house, he dismounted and ascended the hill on foot. Upon his arrival, he found Colonel Rives's command, supported by a portion of Lieutenant Colonel Hull's and Major Milton's command of his division. Price ordered an assault on the position, and Harris, along with Colonel Rives, Colonel Hull and Major Milton, took the Anderson house. During the evening, Union forces retook the house but were again driven out by Harris's men.

Leaving a sufficient force at the Anderson house, Harris descended the hill and moved along the left wing of his command—under Colonel Martin Green, the wing had united with General McBride's command, had driven the Union forces back from an advanced position and was occupying a point with General McBride's command in a trench taken from the Union forces near a mine. Harris ordered Colonel Green to deploy his line to the left and directed that his riflemen should continue to skirmish with the Federal forces, while his men armed only with shotguns, being out of range, should protect themselves beneath the crest of a hill and prepare themselves for any assault from the Union lines. Harris directed Lieutenant Colonels Brace and Hull to move with their commands to the support of Green's position and to extend the flank to the left on Colonel Green's front.

At 7:00 p.m. on September 18, Harris expected the Union forces to attack the Anderson house and create a diversion while Union forces planned to land reinforcements and burn steamers captured by Confederate forces during the day. Price sent Harris reinforcements from General Alexander Steen's division, commanded by Majors Thornton and Winston, and the battery of Captain Kelly. Harris posted the infantry to strengthen the Anderson house, and the artillery was placed to command the wharf and the river. Colonel Congreve Jackson loaned Harris the use of a battalion commanded by Colonel Bevier, which he posted to cover the artillery.

On September 19, Harris moved Colonel Angus MacDonald's command to the extreme left. Harris ordered his sharpshooters to keep up a random fire along his entire front and directed the line of crude field fortifications. The commands of Colonel Green and Lieutenant Colonels Hull and Brace improved their defense. Harris directed that 132 bales of hemp be used as fortifications. He instructed them to wet the bales in the river to protect them against the fire of Union and Confederate troops, but the soggy bales became too heavy to roll into place on the hill. Harris then decided to wet the hemp bales after they were put in place.

At 5:00 p.m., a truce was granted to the Federals to remove their wounded and sick from the Anderson house. The truce allowed Harris to make his final and complete arrangements for the defense of the house. Lieutenant Colonels Hull and Brace were able to improve their defenses, which were composed of earthworks and timber.

At 8:00 a.m. on September 20, Harris ordered more hemp bales to extend the defenses at the position occupied by Colonel Green and Lieutenant Colonels Hull and Brace. He ordered the bales to be used as breastworks, to be pushed forward toward the Union lines in parallel approaches. Union forces opened up with artillery and rifle fire, but Harris's men continued to approach the Union forces, pouring into their ranks a destructive fire until 2:00 p.m., when Union forces surrendered. Harris captured 3,500 Union soldiers. During the battle, Harris lost 11 men killed, 18 severely wounded and 26 slightly wounded, for a total of 55 casualties.

After the Battle of Lexington, Harris became a member of the Confederate Congress in Richmond, Virginia. He was a member of the House Military Affairs Committee. Harris was anti-administration and opposed all tax bills. In 1864, he declined to run for a second term in Congress and stayed in the Confederate capital. The Confederate government contracted him to supply the army with needed equipment, which Harris purchased from European suppliers and shipped through in Union blockade runners. When Richmond fell in April 1865, Harris tried to flee the country but was captured on May 17, 1865, in Florida and imprisoned at Fort McHenry in Baltimore, Maryland. Harris refused to take the oath of allegiance. After being pardoned, he went to Honduras and the Yucatan, where he remained for about a year. During his stay, he was given command of troops, but he did not like the countries so he left for Paris, France. He returned to America after Reconstruction. Harris returned to Missouri and worked for the New York Life Insurance Association of America in St. Louis and opened an office in Texas in 1870. He settled in New Orleans and helped establish the *Times-Democrat*.[134]

When he moved to Kentucky, he was a member of the Kentucky state legislature a number of times and was assistant secretary of state under Governor Luke Blackburn. He made the reputation as being one of the most efficient assistant secretaries of state Kentucky had ever had. His last public office was as a member of the Kentucky legislature from Oldham County, which he held from 1885 to 1886. In 1887, he was sent by Governor Simeon Buckner to represent the state at the Centennial of the Constitution Convention in Philadelphia.[135]

After moving to Kentucky, he traveled to Lexington, Missouri, on October 4, 1891—the only time he ever attended a reunion of Confederate and Union soldiers from the battle. He represented the Confederate soldiers, and Colonel McNulta was appointed as representative of the Whiskey Trust, which represented the Union soldiers. General Harris took a prominent role in the reunion and helped to assemble the records relating to the battle to make sure the records were preserved for history.[136]

After the death of his first wife, Harris married Mary Wingate, the granddaughter of Dr. Wingate, who was a celebrated physician in Louisville. She died in Cintronelle, Alabama, in 1887, leaving a son, Lucian Harris. Harris proceeded to marry Miss Peck of Lexington. He died on April 8, 1895. His services were held at the Locust Lodge at Pee Wee Valley. His remains were brought to Louisville, and his body was interred at Cave Hill Cemetery.[137]

Chapter 13

Confederate Sergeant Major Joel Womack

Joel Mayo Womack was born on February 3, 1845, in New Orleans, Louisiana. Before the Civil War, he was a cadet at the South Carolina Military Academy, also known as The Citadel. He was detailed as a drillmaster at Camp Butler near Aiken, South Carolina, and helped train the 14th South Carolina Infantry. When the Civil War broke out, he enlisted in Captain Moses B. Humphrey's company of Cadet Rangers and later with 16th Battalion of South Carolina Partisan Rangers, which later became Company F, 6th South Carolina Cavalry.

On June 9, 1862, he transferred to Company D, 5th South Carolina Cavalry.[138] On January 3, 1863, the 5th South Carolina Regiment was commanded by Lieutenant Colonel Samuel W. Ferguson of the 28th Mississippi Cavalry, who was on leave in Charleston recuperating from injuries received when he fell from his horse. Ferguson never rejoined the regiment and instead decided to return to the Western Theater, where he was promoted to brigadier general. Lieutenant Colonel Robert J. Jeffords served as acting commander, but on July 28, 1863, Colonel John Dunovant took over the command. The 5th South Carolina served as detached commands and was assigned to coast defenses at various locations in the Carolinas until March 1864. In March, the War Department ordered the 5th South Carolina to Virginia, where the regiment assembled in April, and along with the 4th and 6th South Carolina Cavalry regiments formed Butler's Brigade, Hampton's Division, Cavalry Corps, Army of Northern Virginia. For the remainder of the year, the regiment was actively engaged as mounted infantry in various

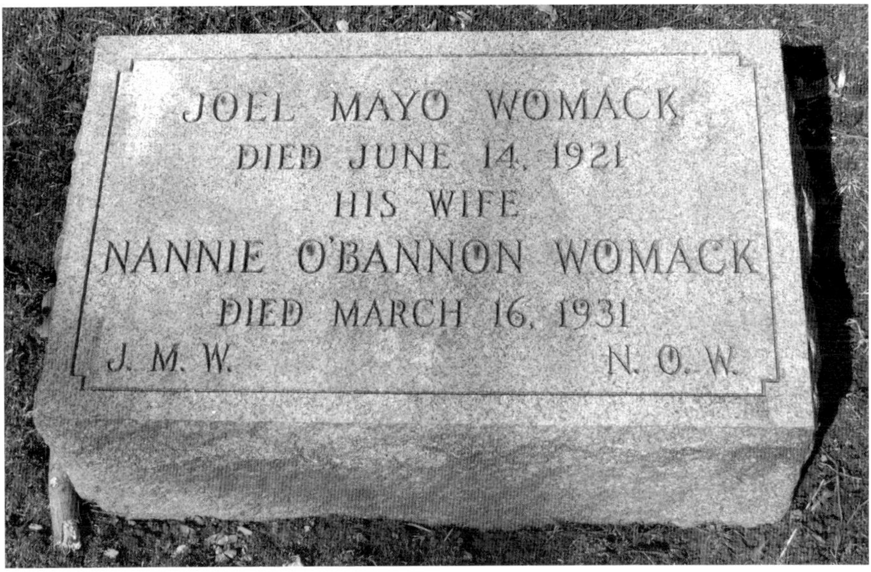

Joel Womack's tombstone, Cave Hill Cemetery, Louisville, Kentucky. *Photograph courtesy of the author.*

actions associated with the defense of Richmond and Petersburg and the vital railroad lines supplying the Army of Northern Virginia.

On June 20, 1864, Womack was captured at White House near Louisa Court House, Virginia, and sent to Point Lookout, Maryland. On July 25, 1864, he was transferred to a prisoner of war camp at Elmira, New York. In May 1864, the United States War Department learned that there were vacant barracks in Elmira. On July 1864, the War Department sent seven hundred Confederate prisoners of war from Point Lookout, Maryland, and other overcrowded prisons, including Womack, to Elmira. By the end of August 1864, there were ten thousand enlisted Confederate prisoners. Living conditions were deplorable since the barracks held only half the prisoners, with the other half living in tents, even in the harsh New York winters. There was also a serious sanitation problem. The sinks drained into a pond that stretched the length of the prison. The forty-acre camp was located below the level of the Chemung River, making drainage of the pond difficult if not impossible. The prison also lacked vegetables, and the prisoners soon came down with scurvy. By November 1, 1864, 775 prisoners died from the disease.

Womack soon had enough of the conditions at Elmira, and on October 27, 1864, he decided to forge Commandant Major Henry Colt's name to a pass that he found in a book in the prison library. He presented the pass to the guards at the front and gate walked out. Womack wrote that "the farther I got away, the faster I walked." He was the eleventh person to escape Elmira.[139] On October 7, 1864, ten other prisoners managed to dig a tunnel sixty-six feet long under the stockade perimeter and escaped.

Womack managed to make his way back to Richmond, Virginia, and rejoined his company. In January 1865, the 5th South Carolina was reassigned to Wheeler's Cavalry Corps, Army of Tennessee, and returned to Columbia, South Carolina, under Lieutenant General Wade Hampton to check the advance of Major General William T. Sherman's troops from Georgia. The 5th Carolina was involved in continuous skirmishing with numerically superior Federal forces as they moved north from Columbia to northeastern South Carolina and finally into central North Carolina. The 5th South Carolina participated in the final battle of the Carolinas Campaign at Bentonville and provided escort to General Joseph Johnston when he met to discuss surrender terms with General Sherman at the William Bennett House near Durham Station, North Carolina, on April 17, 1865. On April 27, 1865, the regiment, along with Womack, surrendered at Hillsboro, North Carolina.

In 1870, Womack moved to Louisville, Kentucky. He was one of the organizers of the Louisville Jockey Club and was the first treasurer. He was also secretary when Churchill Downs was built in 1875. He was a close friend of Meriwether Lewis Clark Jr. and assisted Clark in establishing the Kentucky Derby.[140] He also fought in the Spanish-American War in the Louisville Legion. Under Kentucky Governor Augustus Willson (thirty-sixth governor of Kentucky, 1907–11), Womack was appointed commissioner of Confederate records.[141] In 1917, he was an insurance salesman and later was involved in the lumber business in Costa Rica, where he contracted a tropical disease. He spent several weeks in the hospital and died on June 14, 1921.[142] He was buried in Cave Hill Cemetery. His daughter, Margaret O'Bannon Womack, was an author who wrote *Red Cross Girls*, *Ranch Girls* and *Campfire Girls*, a series of books for young ladies.

Chapter 14

Confederate "Boy Major" Adolphus Richards

Adolphus Richards, also known as "Dandy" Richards at times because of his immaculate uniform, became a Confederate major at the age of twenty-one in Confederate Colonel John S. Mosby's famous 43rd Virginia battalion, also known as Mosby's Partisan Rangers. His career in the Confederate cavalry was one marked by bravery and fearlessness. After the war, Richards's ambition and intellect helped him became one of the leading lawyers in Louisville and a judge.

On May 26, 1844, Adolphus Richards was born in Fauquier County, Virginia, to his parents, Jesse and Eleanor Richards. His father resided in the southeastern part of Loudoun County near the town of Upperville and devoted his life to farming. Adolphus Richards attended the military academy of Upperville, and just before the Civil War broke out, he enrolled at Randolph Macon College. In 1862, he marched from the college campus and entered the Confederate army as a private in Turner Ashby's cavalry. After the death of Ashby, he served as an aide on the staff of Confederate General William "Grumble" Jones, who succeeded General Ashby in command of the cavalry forces in the valley of Virginia. Richards was twice mentioned in the reports of General Jones for gallantry in action. In September 1863, Richards resigned his position on Jones's staff and enlisted as a private in the 43rd battalion of Virginia Cavalry, commanded by the legendary Confederate General John S. Mosby. On December 15, 1863, Richards was promoted to first lieutenant of Company C.

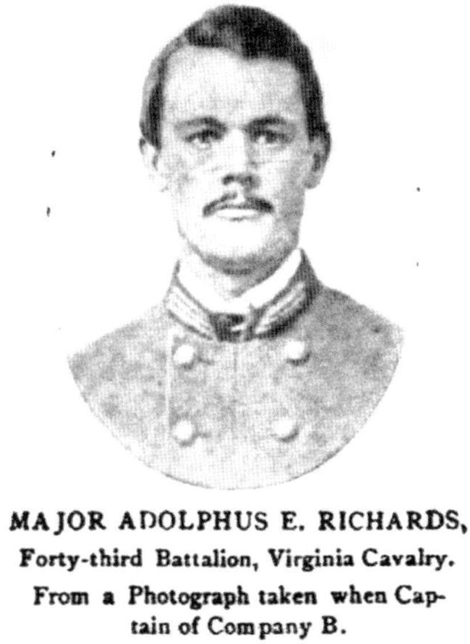

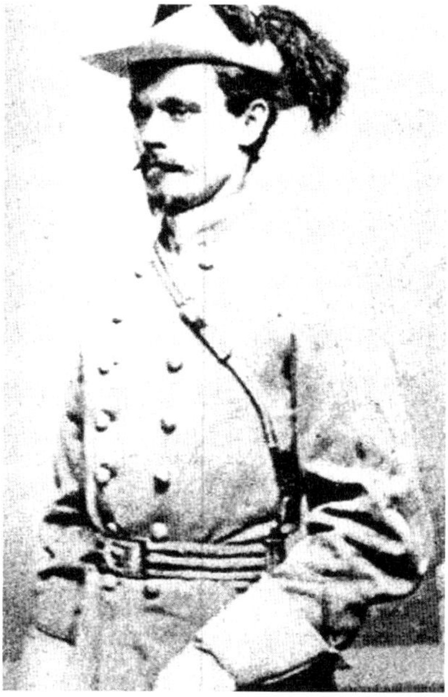

Left: Major Adolphus Richards. *From James Williamson's* Mosby's Rangers: A Record of the Operations of the Forty-Third Battalion Virginia Cavalry *(Ralph Kenyon Publishing, 1896).*

Right: Major Adolphus Richards. *Courtesy of https://cenantua.wordpress.com/2011/09/04/identifying-more-unknowns-mosby-vs-blazers-scouts.*

When the Civil War began, Mosby formed a local cavalry company and fought at the First Battle of Bull Run. He was assigned to General J.E.B. Stuart's cavalry as a scout. Early in the 1862, the Confederate Congress enacted the Partisan Ranger Act, which provided for independent bodies of cavalry to be organized as other government troops. The officers were to be regularly commissioned and the men to be paid like other soldiers. The difference between regular cavalry and partisan rangers was that the rangers would operate independently of the regular army and be entitled to the legitimate spoils captured from the Union army. Mosby had only eight hundred men in his command.[143]

The Army of the Potomac became so harassed by Mosby's Partisan Rangers that it assigned Colonel Richard Blazer in command of Blazer's scouts. Blazer's scouts had just one mission: engage in anti-guerrilla activity. On February 1864, General George Crook, who commanded the Kanawha District, wanted to expand the size and focus of the Union scouts, including Blazer's scouts. When Union General Phil Sheridan moved his command to

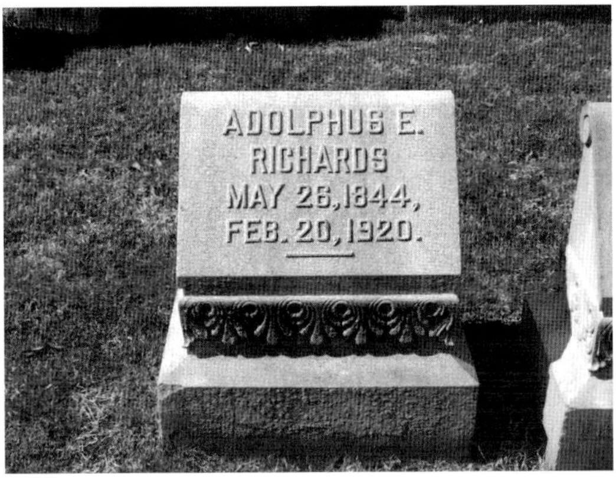

Major Adolphus Richards's tombstone, Cave Hill Cemetery. *Photograph taken by the author.*

the Shenandoah Valley, he was harassed by partisan bands operating in the region. Mosby literally brought Sheridan's movements to a stop. General Sheridan wanted a scouting force whose only mission was to destroy Mosby. Crook recommended Blazer. Blazer's men were armed with one hundred Spencer repeating rifles, and in the spring of 1864, he set out on his mission to destroy Mosby.[144]

On April 26, 1864, Richards was promoted by President Jefferson Davis to captain of Company B, 43rd Virginia battalion, for his gallantry and skill displayed in action. On September 3, 1864, Blazer's scouts fought an engagement with Mosby's men at Myer's Ford, Virginia. Blazer's men rode to the ford at the Shenandoah River. They found Mosby's men resting on the west side of the river. Blazer attacked and scattered the force, but fearing reinforcements, Blazer called off the pursuit and headed back toward the river.[145]

When Mosby learned of his men's defeat at Myer's Ford, he became enraged. Mosby assigned Richards two companies of Partisan Rangers with the purpose to "wipe Blazer out." Mosby told Richards to "[g]o through him! You let the Yankees whip you, I'll get hoop skirts for you! I'll send you into the first Yankee regiment we come across." On November 19, 1864, Richards rode out in search of Blazer. The Rangers heard that Blazer was in Kabletown, West Virginia. Richards told his men to quickly ride in that direction.

When Richards reached the town, he discovered that Blazer's men had recently left. Richards knew that Blazer had to be close, so he began a search. Blazer was also searching for Mosby's force. The next day, the two opposing forces found each other just seven miles west of Snicker's Gap. Richards drew up in line of battle and awaited Blazer's approach. Blazer heralded his advent with a shower of bullets and then rushed down the road. Richards, instead of awaiting Blazer's approach, decided to meet Blazer head-on. At fifty yards, Richards ordered a charge. Blazer discovered his error too late. Blazer had 62 men, and Richards had at least 110 men. Richards closed in on Blazer's scouts, who lost a third of their men in the initial attack. Blazer's men were only armed with Spencer rifles, which were not suited for close combat. Richards's men were armed with Colt revolvers, perfect for short range. Blazer's scouts were soon completely routed and fled to Myerstown, West Virginia. Blazer lost 30 men captured and 30 men killed. Richards only lost 1 man killed and 5 slightly wounded. After the battle, Blazer's scouts ceased to exist as a military force.[146]

On December 6, 1864, at the age of twenty-one, Richards was promoted to major of the battalion "for valor and skill on many occasions." He continued to ride with Mosby's Rangers until the end of the war. After the Civil War, Richards returned to Virginia and was a student at the University of Virginia for two years. His professional education was completed at the University of Louisville, and in the spring of 1868, he was admitted to the bar in Louisville. His first partnership was with Lee C. Woolfolk, who was county attorney, and later with General Basil Duke, who was later commonwealth attorney. In 1882, he was honored with the nomination for judge of the superior court on the Democratic ticket and elected for a four-year term. In 1886, he was a member of the firm of Richards and Harris. He later entered into a partnership with Royal Weissinger and John Baskin under the name of Richards, Weissinger and Baskin.

As city attorney, Richards framed the laws creating the board of water works and served as the attorney for the Louisville Water Company. He also was one of the organizers of the Louisville and Atlantic Railroad Company, and under his direction, the line flourished and was extended. The Louisville and Atlantic was sold in 1909 to the Louisville and Nashville Railroad. He was appointed attorney for the receiver of the Louisville and Interurban Company and aided in the readjustment, improvement and extension of the properties of the company; he also assisted in the company's sale to the Louisville Railway Company.[147]

He was a member of the United Confederate Veterans and was a member of the board of trustees of the Kentucky State Confederate Home at Pee Wee Valley. He was a director of the Columbia Fidelity Trust Company and a member of the Pendennis Club.[148]

On May 11, 1870, Richards married Mattie Tyler and had two children, John Tyler and Jesse Richards Ronald. Richards died on February 20, 1920, and was buried at Cave Hill Cemetery. H. Levin, who published *Lawyers and Lawmakers of Kentucky*, stated that Richards had "liberal intellectual endowments and great moral courage, broad culture in literature, he is fully equipped for the science of law, which is almost limitless in its possibilities. He has ever the courage of his convictions and his justice and fairness to others has won him the highest respect of all."[149]

Chapter 15

Confederate Medical Director David Wendel Yandell

David Wendel Yandell was born on September 4, 1826, in Murfreesboro, Tennessee. His family later moved to Nashville, Tennessee, and when his father took a position to teach at Transylvania University in Lexington, Kentucky, the family moved to that state. In 1837, the family moved to Louisville. David Yandell entered the new Louisville Medical Institute and earned his degree as a medical doctor. In April 1851, he married Frances Jane Crutcher. David eventually became chairman of the Clinical Medicine and Pathological Anatomy at the Louisville Medical Institute.

When Kentucky's neutrality was shattered in September 1861, David applied for and was immediately granted a commission in the Confederate medical department. He resigned from the Louisville Medical Institute and left for Nashville, Tennessee, to join the Provisional Army of the Confederate States. David traveled between Bowling Green, Kentucky, which was Confederate General Albert Sidney Johnston's headquarters, and Nashville. By mid-October 1861, Yandell had been assigned to General Johnston, commander of the Army of the West. Johnston appointed Yandell the medical directorship of the Army of the West.

After the fall of Fort Henry and Fort Donelson in February 1862, Yandell, along with Confederate General Albert Sidney Johnston's army, withdrew from Kentucky and fell back to Corinth, Mississippi. In April 1862, Johnston's army moved on Union General Ulysses Grant's army. During the attack, Johnston told Yandell to take care of the Union and Confederate wounded. Johnston was riding his horse, Fire-Eater, while leading his men

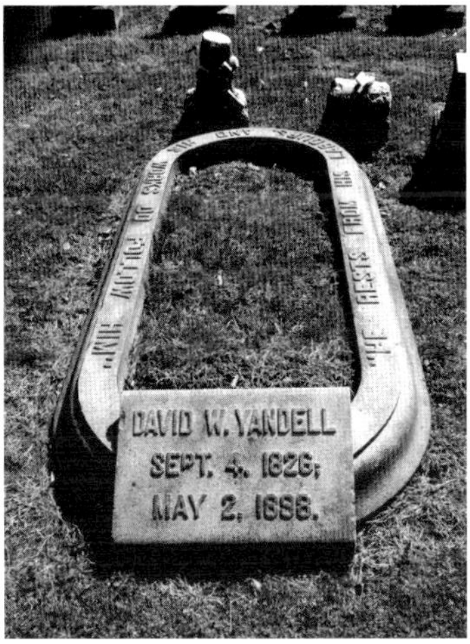

Dr. David Yandell's tombstone, Cave Hill Cemetery. *Photograph taken by the author.*

through the Peach Orchard when he was struck four times by Minié bullets. One of the bullets landed behind his right leg, and his blood flowed into his boot. No one knew that Johnston had been seriously wounded. Governor of Tennessee Isham Harris and Captain W.L. Wickham helped Johnston dismount from his horse. Captain Theodore O'Hara, Johnston's aide, and Colonel William Preston Johnston rode up and found General Johnston on the ground. Johnston took his last breath in Preston's arms. Ironically, Yandell had supplied tourniquets to all commanders in the field, including Johnston, but since Yandell was away helping wounded soldiers, no one knew how to use them.

After Johnston's death, Yandell was assigned as medical director for Confederate General William Hardee's Corps and made president of the Army of Tennessee's Board of Medical Examiners. During the Confederate invasion of 1862, Yandell rode into Kentucky along with Hardee's Corps. After the Battle of Perryville on October 8, 1862, Confederate General Braxton Bragg led the army out of Kentucky and back into Tennessee. The army's retreat led to criticism from not only the soldiers who fought at the Battle of Perryville but also Bragg's officers. Yandell called the failed invasion "Bragg's terrible blunder." Yandell wrote to Colonel William Preston, aide to Jefferson Davis, that he should visit the Army of Tennessee and gather the facts and opinions of the Kentucky campaign. Yandell wrote to Johnston that Bragg "was either stark mad or utterly incompetent." Yandell also wrote that Confederate General Leonidas Polk, who was an Episcopal bishop before the war and one of the Bragg's corps commanders, could "do more service on a chronic court of inquiry than in command of troops." Yandell stated that if "Bragg isn't removed and Polk transferred to house duties, we will all go to the devil out here. Providence alone saved us in Kentucky and that in spite of the commander."[150]

On December 14, 1862, Confederate General John Hunt Morgan, "the Thunderbolt of the Confederacy," married Mattie Ready at the Ready family mansion in Tennessee. The wedding was to be the event of the season. General Morgan had also just been promoted to brigadier general. General

Leonidas Polk, with his vestments covering his general's uniform, performed the ceremony. Mattie Ready's brother, Horace, an officer in General Hardee's staff, and Colonel George St. Leger Grenfell served as groomsmen. Generals Bragg, Hardee, Ben Cheatham and John Breckinridge looked on. An elaborate dinner was served after the wedding.[151]

After the dinner, a group of officers was having wine in the library when someone suggested that Yandell perform his popular impersonations of senior officers. He did Polk and was finishing Hardee when Bragg was called from the room. Yandell's best impression was of Bragg. The officers in the room pleaded for Yandell to do Bragg. Yandell began, striding to and fro, scowling, waving his arms and rasping out jerky sentences on two of Bragg's favorite themes: lack of discipline and use of whiskey in the army. Suddenly, Bragg walked back into the room and Yandell stopped, his face turning pale. Bragg then spoke in the silent room, "Go on, doctor, don't let me interrupt you. It is certainly entertaining and doubtless quite accurate."[152] Yandell did not repeat the impression.

Yandell remained with Hardee throughout the winter and early spring of 1863. At the Battle of Stone's River, which was fought between December 31, 1862, and January 2, 1863, Confederate General Roger Hanson, a commander under Confederate General John Breckinridge's Orphan Brigade, was seriously wounded. He was taken to Murfreesboro by wagon. When he arrived at the Haynes house, Mary Breckinridge cut off Hanson's boot and tore off pieces of her dress to make bandages. Roger Hanson's wife, Virginia, was understandably distraught and worked with Breckinridge to make her husband more comfortable. Yandell examined Hanson and decided that he was too weak for a leg amputation. Hanson told Yandell to "do the best for me, doctor." Yandell told Hanson he did not think the general would survive. On January 4, 1863, Hanson died.[153]

After the Battle of Murfreesboro, Yandell was transferred to Jackson, Mississippi, and served under General Joseph Johnston. In 1864, Yandell was transferred to Louisiana and served under Confederate General Edmund Kirby Smith, who was commander of the Army of the Trans-Mississippi, as his medical director. On June 6, 1865, Yandell surrendered in New Orleans, Louisiana. Yandell returned to Louisville.[154]

After the war, David, along with his father and brother, opened a small office on Chestnut Street. In 1867, Yandell rejoined the University of Louisville as a professor of clinical medicine and two years later became professor of clinical surgery. He also became an active senior editor of one of the Midwest's leading medical journals, the *American Practitioner*, and was an advocate for a professional society that both aided in the dissemination of knowledge and worked to improve the profession's standards. On May 8, 1898, David Yandell was laid to rest at Cave Hill Cemetery. With his death, the medical community lost a man who helped mold and direct medical education in the nineteenth century.[155]

Chapter 16

Confederate Major John Leathers

John Leathers was born on April 27, 1841, in Middleway, Northern Virginia, now West Virginia. He was the son of a cabinetmaker and the youngest of seven children. While working for his father, he learned the skills of writing bills of sale, delivering invoices and keeping inventory, all of which would serve him well later in his life. By age sixteen, Leathers was working at a dry goods store in Martinsburg, Virginia.[156]

In 1859, Leathers moved from Virginia to Louisville, Kentucky, to work for his uncle, who was a local retail druggist. One year later, Leathers became a bookkeeper in the wholesale clothing firm of William Terry & Company.[157] When the Civil War broke out, Leathers decided to return home to Virginia and joined Company D, 2nd Virginia Infantry, Stonewall Jackson's brigade, of Confederate General Robert E. Lee's Army of Northern Virginia. In 1862, Leathers was promoted to sergeant major.

At the Battle of Gettysburg, Leathers received a severe wound. He was hospitalized on August 8, 1863, at Charlottesville, Virginia. He returned to his command on August 21, 1863. He was listed as a prisoner of war in Spotsylvania Court House, Virginia, in May 1864, and by May 19, 1864, he was a prisoner at the infamous Point Lookout, Maryland. He was exchanged on February 13, 1865.[158] He decided that his fighting career in the Civil War was over and returned to Louisville. In 1865, he joined the firm of Jones & Tapp. On March 12, 1869, he married Kate Armstrong of Louisville. In 1870, he became a partner and renamed the company to Tapp, Leathers and Company.[159]

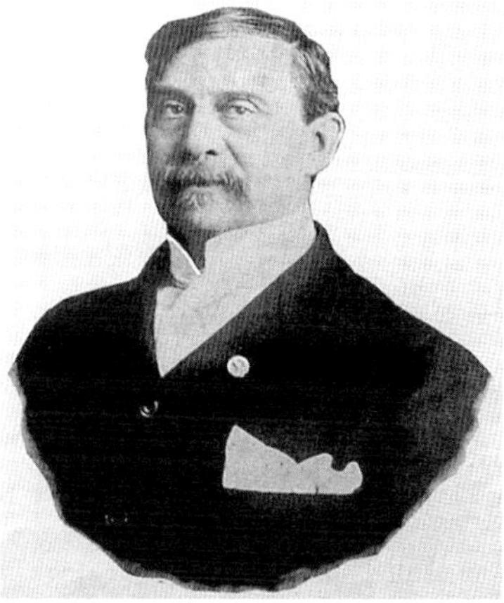

John Leathers. *Courtesy of the Old Bardstown Village Inc. Photograph taken by the author.*

Throughout the 1870s and 1880s, Leathers managed the operations of Tapp, Leathers and Company. By 1885, he had five hundred employees and manufactured Kentucky jeans and lines of men's and boys' dress clothing for retailers throughout the country. In 1878, he organized Company C of the Louisville Legion, and his men elected him captain.

On April 1, 1885, Theodore Harris moved his Louisville Banking Company to Fifth and Market. Harris hired Leathers to oversee the day-to-day operations of the Louisville Banking Company. Within three years, Leathers had tripled the deposits of the Louisville Banking Company and become head of Kentucky's largest financial institution.[160]

Leathers became a wealthy man, but he used his money toward a multitude of philanthropic endeavors. He attended the Blue and Gray reunions at Gettysburg and in 1913 was appointed treasurer to help raise $500,000 to build the Gettysburg Peace Memorial. Because of his efforts in promoting peace after the war, the Army of the Potomac, an organization composed of officers who served in the Union army, made Leathers an honorary member. Leathers became the only Confederate soldier to ever to be given the honor.

He was also founder of the Masonic Widows and Orphans Home and the Old Masons Home in Shelbyville. For twenty-seven years, he was president of the old Louisville Industrial School, which in 1920 was merged with the Parental Home into the Louisville and Jefferson County Children's Home. He was also president of the Kentucky Humane Society and a member of the board of visitors at the Kentucky Military Institute.

Leathers was also president of the Confederate Association of Kentucky. The group's promise was to "pay a decent respect to the remains and to the memory of those who die."[161] The organization raised $7,500, which went toward relief and memorial work. Leathers gave serious consideration to help any Confederate veteran who was in need. For example, an ex-Confederate soldier named Sergeant Billy Beasley came to Leathers in 1889 seeking help for him and his daughter. Beasley was injured in the Battle of the Wilderness and could barely walk. Leathers gave him a $2 stipend to help him and his daughter, a free apartment for six months and a $100 loan to open a cigar stand on the corner of Fifth and Market. When Beasley died in 1898, Leathers personally met the hearse carrying Beasley's casket at the entrance to Cave Hill Cemetery. Leathers paid for Beasley's funeral, cemetery plot, floral arrangements and headstone.[162]

Leathers continued to help his fellow ex-Confederate soldiers by becoming president of one of the largest United Confederate Veterans camps in the county. He was also instrumental in helping to establish a Confederate Veterans Home on 421 East Chestnut Street in Louisville.[163]

On June 29, 1923, Leathers's long career in business and philanthropy came to an end. He was survived by his wife, Katie Armstrong, and his three sons, Charles, John and Stuart. He was laid to rest at Cave Hill Cemetery in the Confederate section.

Chapter 17

Confederate Captain Pinkney Varble

Pinkney "Pink" Varble was born near Salisbury, South Carolina, on September 8, 1828. He was the son of Henry and Alia Catha Varble. His parents moved to Kentucky in 1831 in wagons and settled in Oldham County near Westport, Kentucky. Pink Varble remained on the family farm until 1842, when he moved to Louisville and was hired to haul wood on a wagon for J.M. Collins. He remained with Mr. Collins for three months and obtained another job with Falls pilot Eli Vansickle. He worked for Mr. Vansickle for six months and then made a contract with him to work four years for his board, clothing and three months' schooling each winter learning the Falls.

On his second year, he took charge of the business, which was buying and selling flatboats and lumber. Before his contract expired with Vansickle, Varble established a ferry line between Portland and New Albany, Indiana. He took charge and ran the boats for two years and then sold his business and kept a boat. Varble was paid $400 per year to run his boat up the Salt River to bring out pig iron. In the fall of 1851, he found a purchaser for his boat. He sold his business, moved to Vicksburg, Mississippi, and opened a coal yard for J.H. Mulford of New Orleans, Louisiana. In April 1852, he decided to return to Louisville, Kentucky. On April 28, 1852, he married Frances Littrell of Ghent, Kentucky.[164]

In September 1853, Captain Varble was elected by the Louisville City Council to the office of Falls pilot. To "shoot the Falls" was harrowing experience, and only a few pilots could accomplish the feat. The *Louisville-*

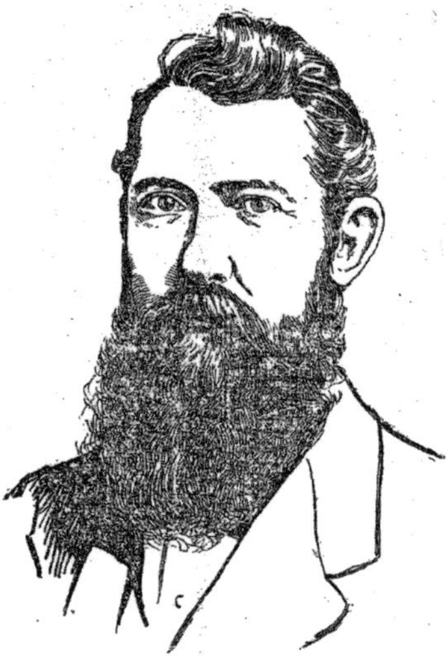

Pinkney Varble. *Courtesy of* Louisville Courier Journal.

Courier Journal reported a story in 1868 that described Varble taking a steamboat over the Falls. The mammoth freight steamer *Thompson Dean* had arrived at the port for the purpose of taking advantage of the rise in the river in order to get over the Falls. The channel known as the middle chute, the only navigable one, was very narrow, only forty-eight feet in width and rimmed with sharp, dangerous reefs on either side—a boat would be smashed to pieces by the swift current from the slightest deviation from the channel. The *Dean* was fifty-one feet wide. The seeming impossibility of navigating a boat of that width through a channel of forty-eight feet was accomplished by listing or careening the ship until it drew three feet, nine inches on the starboard side, enabling the starboard knuckle to pass over the right-hand reef. Varble was able to successfully accomplish the task, and the steamer passed through the narrow channel, only rubbing slightly in one or two places, and all without injuring or straining the boat. Later that afternoon, Varble successfully accomplished two other feats in piloting, almost if not quite as difficult as what he had just done with the *Dean*. He brought up towboats, the *Simpson Horner* and *Alps*, each drawing four feet. He took the Simpson over the channel in one hour and twenty minutes and the *Alps* in fifty minutes from the time of starting until the boats landed.[165]

In 1859, Varble built the towboat *Pink Varble*, and in 1860, he built the *Charles Miller*. On April 12, 1861, the Civil War began when Fort Sumter in Charleston Harbor was fired on by Confederate forces under Confederate General P.G.T. Beauregard. On May 16, 1861, Kentucky declared its neutrality. On September 3, 1861, Kentucky's neutrality was shattered when Confederate forces under Confederate General Leonidas Polk invaded the state and took Columbus, Kentucky. Confederate General Albert Sidney Johnston took Bowling Green, Kentucky, and set up his headquarters. Confederate General Felix Zollicoffer took the Cumberland Gap area. With the Civil War breaking out in Kentucky, Varble continued to do business with both the Union and Confederacy. In 1861, he towed fifty streetcars on barges to New Orleans, the first used in the city, after he secured a permit from the

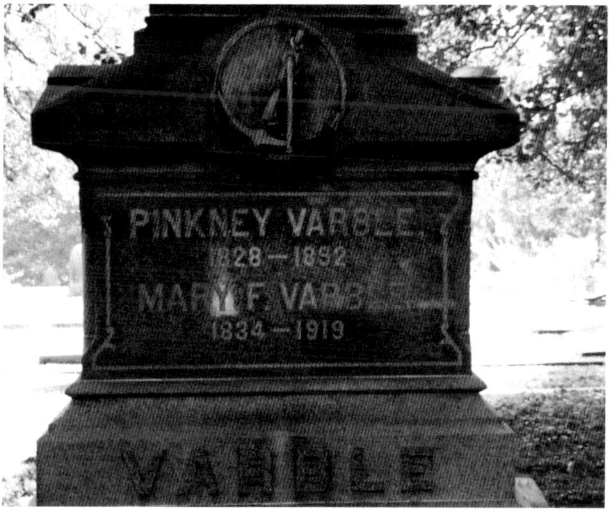

Pinkney Varble Monument, Cave Hill Cemetery. *Photograph taken by the author.*

Confederate secretary of war to go through the lines. He also secured the proper papers to come back through the lines to return to Kentucky. The papers read, "By authority of President of Confederate States of America, the steamer *Charles Miller* is permitted to pass into the United States without molestation." The papers were signed by Governor Moore of Louisiana.[166]

In November 1861, Captain Pink Varble transported a barge towed by his ship *Pink Varble* containing one hundred tons of mill machinery for spinning and weaving cotton. The boxes contained eighty cotton looms for manufacturing of common domestic fabric. The looms were made in Paterson, New Jersey, and valued at $50,000. The looms had been waiting for three months in Louisville until the permits were secured to haul the machinery to Confederate Tennessee. Varble towed the barge from Louisville to the mouth of the Cumberland River and then up the Cumberland into the state of Tennessee to the McMinnville Manufacturing Company in McMinnville.[167]

On December 25, 1861, the *Pink Varble* left Nashville , and when it arrived in Dover, Tennessee, Confederate authorities arrested Daniel Richards, Barney Seales, Daniel McLaughlin, Captain William Varble (Pink Varble's brother), George Dickinson and William Broin along with five deckhands. The men were jailed for twenty-seven hours and regarded with suspicion. The men were later transported to Nashville. After several days in jail, Confederate General Albert Sidney Johnston allowed the men to return to Louisville. On January 3, the men were transported by the *Sunny Side* back to Louisville. Captain William Varble was not allowed to bring back the *Pink Varble* through Confederate lines. General Johnston reported that the Confederate government would pay Captain Pink Varble for the loss of his ship.[168] With the blockade and the seizure of his ship, Varble would no longer work with the Confederacy.

On February 14, 1862, Union General Ulysses S. Grant attacked Fort Donelson on the Cumberland River. Several days later, on February 16, Confederate General Simeon B. Buckner surrendered Fort Donelson along with ten thousand Confederate soldiers. On February 14, 1862, Union General William Nelson's division marched forty-three miles to the confluence of the Salt and Ohio River at West Point, Kentucky. Twenty-five steamboats transported his men to the Cumberland River at Smithland, Kentucky. Captain Varble commanded the *Diana*, which was the flagship for Nelson's command. Nelson arrived at Smithland, and he was ordered to return to Paducah. When he arrived at Paducah, Grant ordered Nelson to come up the Cumberland River to meet him at Fort Donelson.

On February 23, ten steamboats, along with the *Diana*, left with Nelson's men to Fort Donelson. Grant ordered Nelson to take Nashville. Nelson returned to the *Diana* and immediately ordered the flotilla toward Nashville. On February 25, Nelson reached the abandoned Fort Zollicoffer. High water covered the lower part of Nashville, and the *Diana* docked at the foot of a street between two huge warehouses. The men disembarked from the ships, and Mayor Richard Cheatham surrendered the city.[169] After the fall of Fort Donelson, Captain Varble used the famous *Jacob Strader* to transport sick and wounded soldiers to Louisville military hospitals.[170]

Several months later, in August 1862, Confederate forces under Confederate General Braxton Bragg, commanding the Army of the Mississippi, and Confederate General Edmund Kirby Smith, commanding the Army of East Tennessee, invaded Kentucky. On August 30, Union forces totaling nine thousand men under General Mahlon Mason engaged Confederate General Edmund Kirby Smith's ten thousand men. Confederate forces forced the Federals to retreat, and the retreat eventually became a rout. The Confederates captured six thousand Union prisoners. With the defeat at Richmond, Kentucky, the Union army had no substantial force in Kentucky to take on Confederate General Braxton Bragg or Edmund Kirby's forces. Union General Don Carlos Buell's army managed to avoid a major engagement with Bragg's forces and made its way to Louisville.

Once Buell and the remnants of the troops from Richmond were in Louisville, the Federal government quickly began to reorganize the Union army. Reinforcements and supplies were needed in order to take on Bragg's and Smith's troops. Bragg had orders to take Louisville and hoped that Smith would join his force in Bardstown. The Union army decided to build a pontoon bridge across the Ohio River and another pontoon bridge at Paducah. At the time, there was no bridge that connected Louisville to Indiana. Captain Varble assisted the Union government in building a pontoon bridge at Paducah and Louisville. Once the pontoon bridge had been built across the Ohio, thousands of Union reinforcements and supplies flowed into Louisville. By the end of September 1862, 100,000 Union soldiers occupied the city. On October 2, 1862, the newly formed Army of the Ohio, with 58,000 men under the command of Union General Don Carlos Buell, marched out of Louisville. On October 8, 1862, the Battle of Perryville resulted in a strategic win for the Union army, and Bragg's troops left the state of Kentucky, never to return.

During the Civil War, Captain Varble built thirty-seven barges for the Union government and built and bought thirty steamboats, including the *T.D. Horner*, the *Robert Fulton*, the *Nashville*, the *Greyhound* and the *Falls Pilot*. Many of the boats were either sold to the Union government or were under charter. Varble eventually owned or built fifty-seven steamboats. He continued to transport Union troops until the end of the Civil War. After the Civil War, Varble and Colonel W.J. Mar continued to operate a line of thirteen boats that ran on the Tennessee and White Rivers. Unfortunately, the Civil War had depreciated the value of steamboats, and in 1877, Varble sold the business. Afterward, Varble took up the profession of Falls pilot. During his career, he took more tonnage and more boats over the Falls in safety than any other captain living at that time.

On March 26, 1892, Captain Varble boarded the *John A. Wood*, which was one of the largest towboats on the Ohio River. He was to carry the steamer and large tow over the Falls. The vessel and tow were taken through the Indiana chute and had reached a point midway between the dam and the Louisville bridge when the regular pilot, who had one side of the wheel, saw Captain Varble, who had the other, stagger as though he was about to fall. The pilot leaned over and asked him what was the matter. Varble staggered again and would have fallen if the second pilot had not sprung up to help him. The boat was in the rapids, but several men were in the wheelhouse and held the wheel. Although very ill, Varble remained on the pilothouse sofa and directed the course of the boat through the Falls. A landing was made at Portland, and Varble was transported to the harbor boat *Transit*, which had assisted the *Wood*. He was placed in a cabin bed, and the *Transit* quickly steamed to the main wharf at the foot of Third Street.[171] Varble was taken to his home.

On April 3, 1892, Varble passed away at his home at 1423 Everett Avenue. On April 4, his body was taken from his home to Cave Hill Cemetery. Once they reached Cave Hill Cemetery, they placed the casket in the vault. His funeral was attended by the Odd Fellows, as he was a member. The members of the marine fraternity also attended the funeral. The Knights of the Templar gave beautiful floral arrangements, even though Varble was not even a member. The floral designs were profuse and beautiful in design. The vault was literally covered with all kinds of flowers and roses. One of the floral designs comprised flowers that had been made into two immense pilot wheels, each with a broken spoke. Two large floral designs of anchors were also present at the vault. Varble's friend Captain William Shakespeare Hays wrote a poem for his deceased friend:

He was making a trip down the river of life
But he'll never come back any more
For be answered the hail of the Angel of Death
That waved from the "beautiful shore"
He landed while angels assembled and sailed
But they didn't have long there to wait
For Pink rung the gong and let go of the wheel
And went with them up through God's gate.[172]

Varble had eight children, but only four survived by the time of his funeral: Mary, the wife of John A. Stratton; Nelson, a member of the real estate firm of J. Stratton and Company; Pink Varble Jr., a member of S.J. Hobbs & Company and a major in World War I and World War II; and Melvin, who worked for a collection agency. Varble was also survived by his brothers Rush Varble, Richard Varble and William Varble. Several days later, Pink Varble's casket was removed from the vault and placed in the family plot at Cave Hill Cemetery.

Chapter 18

Dr. Norvin Green

Just before the Civil War broke out, there were many new innovations in technology that would play key roles in Kentucky and the country during war. Railroads, the rifled musket and the transcontinental telegraph were all used by both Union and Confederate forces during the Civil War. Norvin Green would play a role in the Western Theater during the war, and after the war, he would become the president of the Western Union.

In 1844, Samuel Morse, the inventor of the telegraph, sent the first message over the thirty-seven-mile telegraph line he had stretched between Washington, D.C., and Baltimore, Maryland. Fifty different companies owned and operated the network of telegraph wires, so messages had to be transferred between companies and then forwarded to their eventual destinations. On October 24, 1861, the transcontinental telegraph reached Sacramento, California, connecting the East Coast and West.[173] Norvin Green changed all that.

Norvin Green was born in New Albany, Indiana, on April 17, 1818. When he was a child, his parents moved to Louisville, Kentucky. His father, Joseph, was a farmer and a veteran of the War of 1812. Green was educated in the local schools. At the age of sixteen, he bought a flatboat and determined to try his luck running a floating grocery store down the Mississippi. His primary customers were lumberjacks. The trip was a success, and he received a good amount of orders that had to be sent by steamboat. His credit was good, and all of his orders were honored. The lumberjacks wanted iron boots, and Green made a profit from selling the

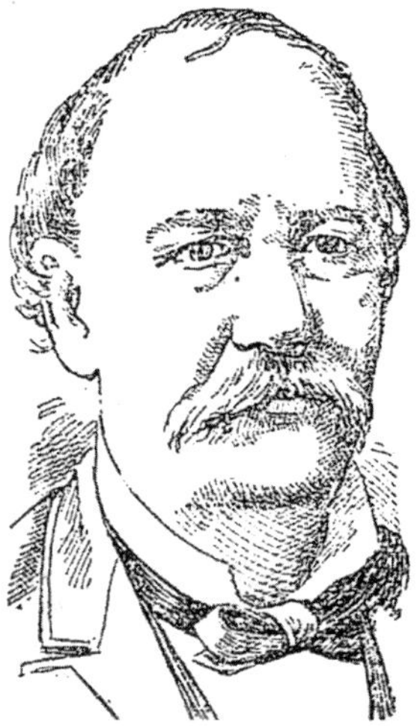

Left: Dr. Norvin Green. *Courtesy of* Louisville Courier Journal.

Below: Close-up of Norvin Green's headstone, Cave Hill Cemetery. *Photograph taken by the author.*

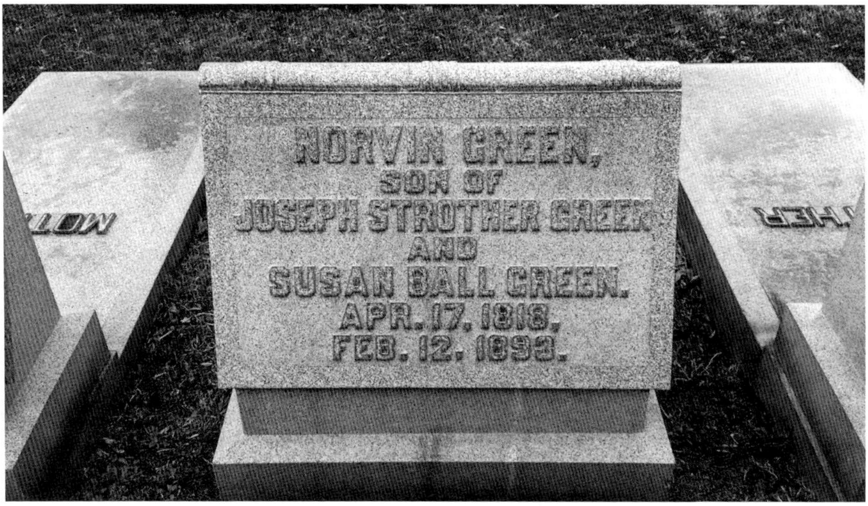

boots. Green also ran a successful business chopping and selling firewood. The money he earned from his businesses allowed him to pay for a medical education. He studied under a local doctor and eventually resumed his studies at the University of Louisville.[174]

In 1840, he graduated from the University of Louisville with his medical degree and started a successful practice. He later became physician of the Western Military Academy in Drennan Springs, Kentucky. He turned his attention to politics and was elected for several terms to the Kentucky legislature. In 1853, he was appointed commissioner of the United

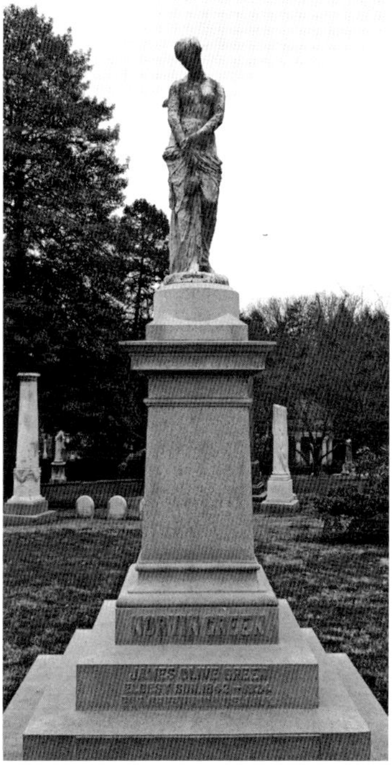

Norvin Green Monument, Cave Hill Cemetery. *Photograph taken by the author.*

States in charge of the construction of the customhouse and post office in Louisville. While engaged in his duties as commissioner, he became one of the lessees of the "United New Orleans and Ohio," also known as the Morse line, and "The People's" telegraph line between Louisville and New Orleans. After he became president of the company, he united the company under the name of the Southern Telegraph Company. Both lines started from Louisville and passed through Nashville into Middle Tennessee, where they divided. The Morse line went to Somerville, Tennessee, with a branch to Memphis, Juanita and Potontoc to Greenville, Mississippi; from there, the lines went down the Walnut Ridge to Vicksburg, Grand Gulf and Natchez to Baton Rouge, Louisiana. The People's line went from Lawrenceburg to Tuscumbia, Alabama, Columbus, Canton, Jackson, Gallatin and Liberty, Mississippi, to Baton Rouge and then to New Orleans. One only needs to look at the names and realize how important these cities would become during the Civil War. After Green consolidated the company into the Southern Telegraph Company, he forever became identified with the history of the telegraph.[175]

The telegraph helped transform warfare. Both the Union and Confederate armies used the telegraph. Telegraph wires enabled field commanders to remain in constant touch with their bases, to learn quickly of changing developments and to rectify shortages of men and materials as they occurred. Telegraphs enabled commanders of armies divided by thousands of miles to coordinate their activities. For the first time, governmental leaders had direct contact with their commanders in the field. Both President Abraham Lincoln and Confederate President Jefferson Davis corresponded with their commanders almost on a daily basis. Reporters from newspapers and magazines kept the public informed about action in the field. The *New York Times* had a Louisville correspondent who used the telegraph wires to keep the East Coast informed about the war in the Western Theater.[176]

Telegraph wires generally ran alongside railroads. The system was privately owned and operated by civilians, and the work of operators was highly prized by both sides. The Union considered telegraphers vital to the functioning of the army, and they were exempted from the draft. Civilian operators played an important role in the operation of field armies, striking their tents and putting their wagons into line when armies moved. In laying and maintaining wires at army and corps headquarters, they faced many of the hazards of combat. Operators suffered causalities of nearly 10 percent, about the same as combat troops. Civilians strung about 15,000 miles of wire and transmitted and received an estimated three thousand messages per day during the war. By 1864, the Union Military Telegraph Service was using more than 6,500 miles of wire, with 76 miles of underwater cable.[177]

Telegraph lines also were used to eavesdrop on and mislead enemy forces. Confederate General John Hunt Morgan took soldier-telegrapher George "Lightning" Ellsworth on raids into Kentucky. Ellsworth learned the tapping habits of other telegraphers and skillfully tapped into Norvin Green's telegraph lines to intercept orders sending Union cavalry and infantry in pursuit of Morgan and to send misleading information on the location of Morgan's raiders. Ellsworth even sent messages between Morgan and chief editor George Prentice of the *Louisville Journal*.[178]

By 1866, the Southern Telegraph Company and the American Telegraph Company were consolidated into the Western Union Telegraph Company. Dr. Green was chosen as vice-president. The Western Union owned seventy-five thousand miles of telegraph line and had eliminated all of its competition.[179] With the exception of about three years, during which Green accepted the presidency of the Louisville, Cincinnati and Lexington Railway Company, he retained the office until January 1873, when he returned to duty as vice-president of the Western Union. In 1878, Green became president of the Western Union. He was also a member of the Telegraphic Mutual Benefit Association and helped to improve the telegraphic service. He was founder of the American Institute of Electrical Engineers, and from 1884 to 1885, he was the organization's first president. He died on February 12, 1893, in his house in Louisville, Kentucky. He amassed a fortune of more than $2 million in stock and real estate. Green was laid to rest at Cave Hill Cemetery.[180]

Norvin Green was a successful doctor and politician, but his contribution to communication with the expansion of the telegraph had an immense impact on the Civil War. Before 1861, troops could only communicate with their field commanders by signal corps or runners on foot or horseback. With the telegraph, field commanders could stay in touch with their superiors in Washington or Richmond. By the time of the Civil War, the telegraph had brought the nation together from East Coast to West. With the Southern Telegraph Company in Louisville, field commanders could telegraph vital information from the field to their commanders in Louisville and from there relay the information to Washington. The Southern Telegraph Company became an integral part of the war in the Western Theater, and the Union army had Norvin Green to thank.

Chapter 19

Washington Wyatt

Washington Wyatt was one of the most successful undertakers in Louisville and was one of the best-known and generally liked men in the city of Louisville. His most memorable period during his career came during the Civil War, when he buried thousands of Union and Confederate soldiers.

Washington Wyatt was born in Cincinnati, Ohio, in 1822, and when he was a boy, he was an apprentice to a cabinetmaker. He spent several years mastering the trade. In 1843, he moved to Louisville, Kentucky, and obtained employment at Smith's undertaking establishment located at Seventh and Market Streets, where he remained for nine years. After working for Smith's, he established a business of his own and secured the building at the southwest corner of Seventh and Jefferson Street.[181]

In 1862, he began to take an interest in steamboat navigation and became part proprietor of several boats running between Louisville and Memphis. His last venture was not very successful, and after sinking a considerable amount of money, he withdrew from the venture and devoted his full time to undertaking.[182]

During his thirty-eight years as an undertaker, he attended twenty thousand coffins on their way to the grave, but the Civil War led to a period when he buried the most coffins in one day. During the war, Wyatt secured a contract with Avery Hospital, located on Fifteenth and Main Streets in Louisville, to supply coffins for Union and Confederate soldiers who died at the hospital. The hospital once belonged to Benjamin F. Avery, who ran a plow works factory at the location, but the Union army took over the building and erected a hospital, which ruined Avery's business.[183]

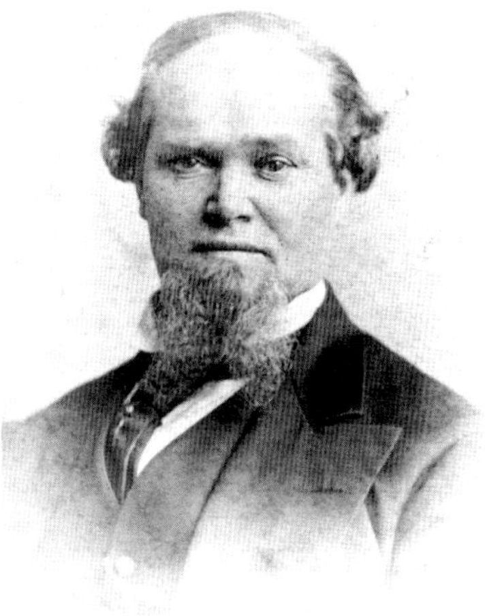

Washington Wyatt. *Courtesy of Jane McCullogh, descendant of Washington Wyatt.*

During the Civil War, Louisville had several Union military hospitals, including the Brown Hospital with 700 beds, the Clay Hospital with 700 beds, the Crittenden Hospital with 360 beds, the Eruptive Hospital with 203 beds, the Foundry Hospital with 200 beds, the Sedgewick General Hospital, the Strader General Hospital, the Transfer General Hospital and the Officer's Hospital with 37 beds. Civil War doctors did not understand germs or how they were carried and transmitted. There was no sterilization of surgical implements. Disease and infection ran rampant among the soldiers. Two-thirds of all soldier deaths that occurred during the Civil War were from disease alone, not from bullets. With so many military hospitals in Louisville, death from infection and disease was a daily occurrence, and someone had to take care of the Civil War dead. Washington Wyatt was one of those caretakers.[184]

Many of the soldiers Washington Wyatt buried were interred at Cave Hill Cemetery. In October 1861, an ordinance was passed by both boards of the Louisville City Council to appropriate a number of acres of ground in Cave Hill Cemetery for the burial of United States troops who fell in the defense of Kentucky and their country.[185] Elijah Huffman and Samuel Hamilton, who were pork packers and pro-Confederate in their sentiments, provided Confederate burial plots in Cave Hill Cemetery.

According to Wyatt, in 1863 he had three hearses running continuously from 6:00 a.m. until 10:00 p.m. He remained at the cemetery and officiated in a hasty ceremony over the graves of the dead soldiers. He buried twenty-eight soldiers in one day alone![186] Wyatt also had private contracts to bury local family members who died during the Civil War and were buried in family plots at Cave Hill Cemetery. The conflict kept Washington Wyatt busy throughout. During the war, Kentucky lost ten thousand men killed in battle and twenty thousand to disease and exposure. Half the Kentuckians

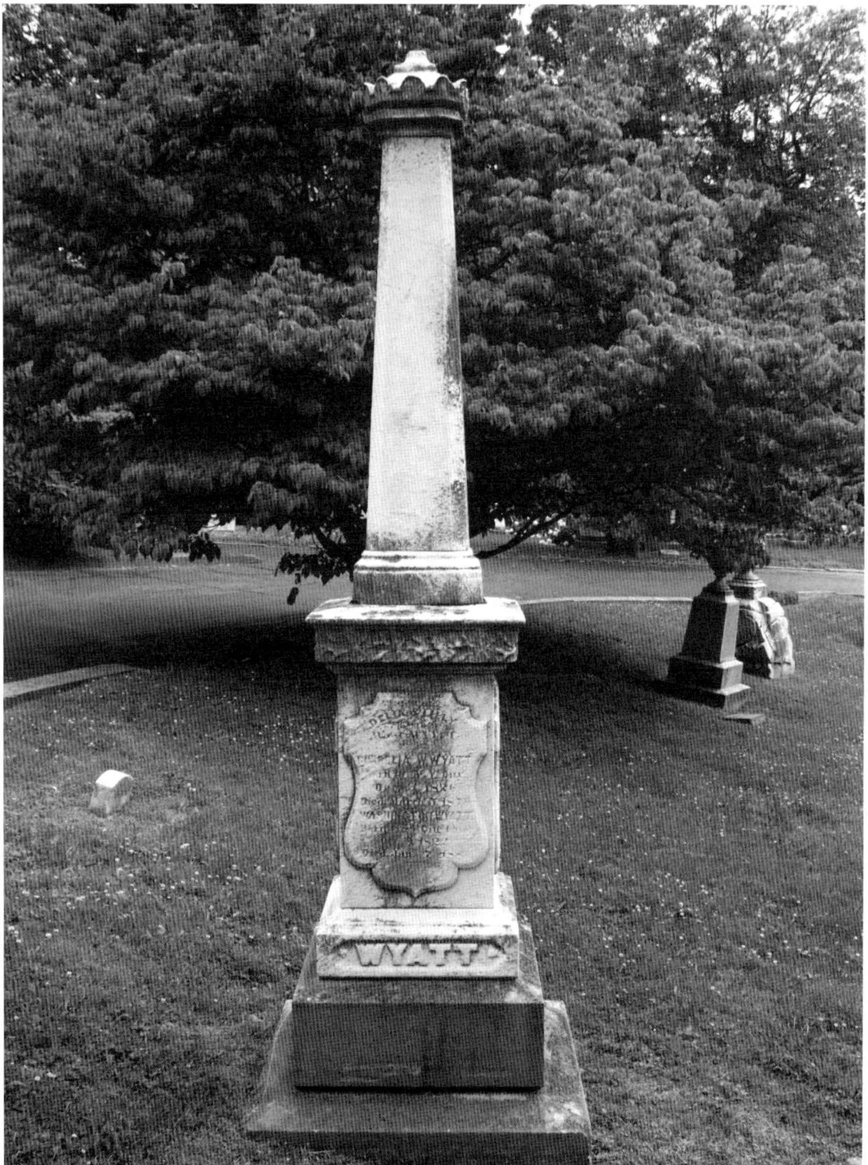

Washington Wyatt Monument, Cave Hill Cemetery. *Photograph taken by the author.*

who reached manhood during the 1850s and early 1860s were either killed or disabled by the war.[187]

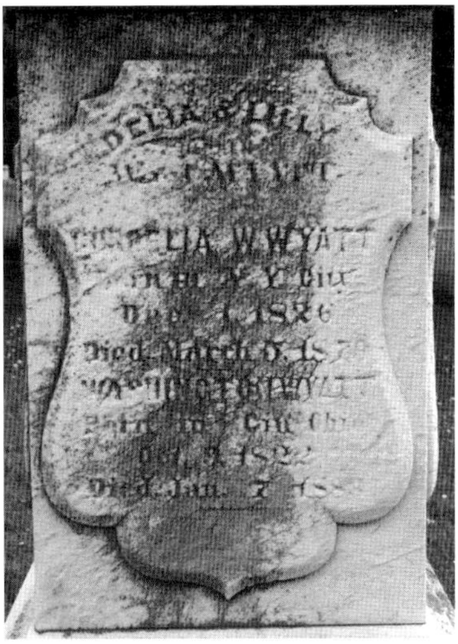

Close-up of Washington Wyatt's monument, Cave Hill Cemetery. *Photograph taken by the author.*

After the Civil War, Wyatt continued to run his undertaking office. He was married and had four children—three daughters and one son. He became a member of the Masons, the Odd Fellows, United Workmen and Knights of Honor. On January 7, 1884, he walked from his room on Jefferson Street to the house where he took his meals at 701 West Jefferson Street. He suddenly became ill and complained of a smothering sensation about his heart. He arose and attempted to walk across the room but staggered and fell to the floor unconscious. The local doctor was summoned, but it was over. His body was taken to his mother's residence on 806 West Chestnut Street for viewing. His wife had died ten years earlier, and his mother, who was eighty, was still alive.[188] Washington Wyatt is buried at Cave Hill Cemetery.

Chapter 20

William Shakespeare Hays

During his lifetime, Colonel William Shakespeare Hays would become a famous songwriter, poet, river editor and a steamboat captain. He was born in Louisville, Kentucky, on July 19, 1837. His father, Hugh Hays, was a leading pioneer plow and wagon manufacturer of the city. As a youth, William Shakespeare Hays was sent to Mrs. Yubank's private school, a famous preparatory institution of learning. After finishing school, he attended Hanover College and later Georgetown University.[189] While at Georgetown, Hays became known as the "boy poet." His first published song was "Little Ones at Home," which was written while he was at Hanover.

After graduating from Georgetown, he began his career on a steamboat. He was first a clerk and moved up to the position of captain, serving both on the Ohio and Mississippi Rivers. Before the Civil War broke out, when John Harney and William Hughes published the *Louisville Democrat*, which later merged with the *Courier* and *Journal*, Hays stopped by the *Louisville Democrat* to see if it would be interested in publishing his articles on riverboat life. When he walked in, the printing press for the *Democrat* broke down, and the paper was to be delayed in publishing. Hays stated he could take a look at the press and see what was wrong, as he learned something about machinery from his father's wagon factory. In a minute, he managed to repair the press. The *Democrat* hired him on the spot, and Hays began publishing his river columns. After the *Democrat* merged with the *Courier-Journal*, he continued as "river editor" of the *Louisville Courier-Journal*. His columns were filled with verse, joke and jingles. While writing for the

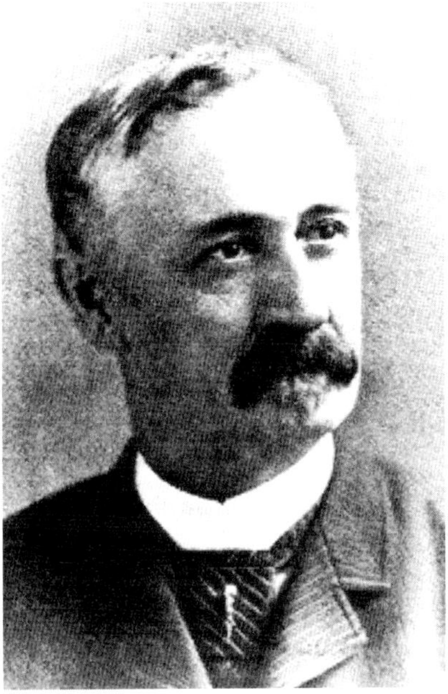

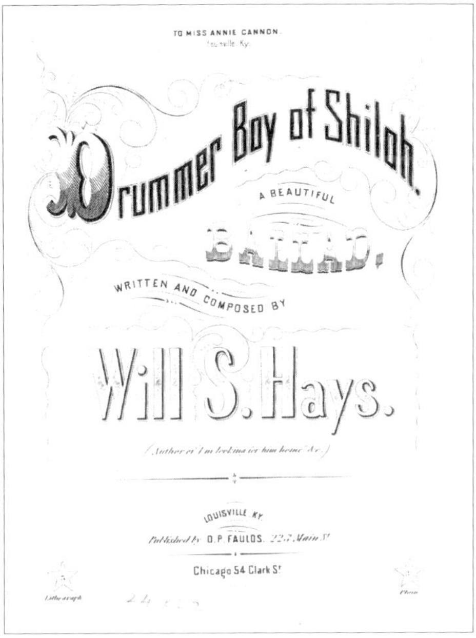

Left: William Shakespeare Hays. *Courtesy of the Library of Congress.*

Right: "Drummer Boy of Shiloh" sheet music. *Courtesy of the Library of Congress.*

newspaper, he began to write songs, and his songs touched a popular chord both North and South.

During the Civil War, he commanded a river transport on the Mississippi between Vicksburg and New Orleans. He also wrote songs such as "Drummer Boy of Shiloh," "McClellan Is the Man," "I Am Dying, Mother, Dying," "Sherman and His Boys" and many others. He was best known for his songs "Evangeline," "Nora O'Neil," "Mollie Darling," "Little Old Cabin in de Lane," Keep in de Middle ob de Road" and "Old Fashioned Roses Are the Sweetest." His song "Mollie Darling" sold more than 2 million copies alone! Amazingly, he sold his music for a sixpence and sold them to minstrel shows.

After the Civil War, during the Reconstruction period, when the country was still torn apart by bitterness toward the South and thousands of Southern families were scattered across the landscape of the United States, William Shakespeare Hays wrote the "Wandering Refugee." Another one of his song that touched on the devastation in the South by the war was his song "My Sunny Southern Home," which helped toward softening and mellowing the feeling of the North toward the South after the war.

After the war, controversy arose as to who wrote the famous song "Dixie." Dan Emmitt claimed that he was the author of the words to "Dixie," but D.F. Faulds, who was one of the leading music publishers in the country, claimed that William Hays wrote the famous lyrics. On May 29, 1898, G.E. Johnson published an article in the *Louisville Courier Journal* on the history of "Dixie" and stated why Hays should be attributed to the writing of the song. Johnson claimed that Hays wrote the words to the music composed by Charles Ward and published by Faulds. Johnson stated that Emmitt sang the song, making the song famous, and changed the words to fit his needs. After the song had attracted some attention, and the Southern troops were being mobilized for war, Hays rewrote the words, making a marching song for the famous Buckner Guards of Louisville.[190]

According to Faulds's story, he stated that "Dixie" was written in 1857 or 1858. He recalled that Charlie Ward entered his office at the age of fifteen in 1854. He was a clerk in his publishing company and slept in the music store. Hays was also a clerk in the same company. Both men aided in Faulds in the publishing business. One afternoon, he received in his mail from New Orleans publishing house a single sheet of music titled "Dixie." When Ward came downstairs the next morning, Faulds gave him the sheet music and asked him to try it on a piano. Faulds stated that the music would make a delightful song and passed the sheet music over to Ward. Hays walked in while Ward was playing the music. Faulds told Hays that he had a new tune that had just come in and wanted him to write some Southern plantation words for the music. While Ward played the music, Hays began writing words to the melody.[191]

In an hour, Hays wrote four or five verses. By nightfall, Ward had arranged the words and Hays sang it while Ward played the music. In two hours, "Dixie" was written, arranged and sung. Faulds claimed that he rushed the song up to the engravers. Shortly after, the song was published by Joe H. McCann, who ran a minstrel show. McCann published the song as "Way Down South in Dixie" and had five thousand copies printed; he sent all the copies to the South. He copyrighted the words, but the music was already common property. Faulds claimed that Dan Emmitt published his version of "Dixie" one year after his publication. Hays's version was strictly a Southern version, whereas Emmitt's version was a version suitable for singing in the North.[192]

Soon after Emmitt's version of "Dixie" was published, Colonel William Pond of the 7th Regiment of New York stated that Faulds had infringed on his copyright of his song, "Dixie." Pond and Faulds decided to leave their dispute to the board of music trade. In 1858, the board met to discuss the issue over the copyright. Six other instrumental editions of "Dixie" were also brought before the board. With so many versions of the song, the board decided not to hear the controversy.[193]

Faulds claimed that he had sold thirty thousand copies of his song before the Civil War, all in the South. His version was being sung in the South before Emmitt's version. Faulds surrendered his plates to Pond. Pond's version was never published in the South, but after the war broke out and Louisville was shut off from the South, Faulds's version of "Dixie" was copyrighted under the Confederate laws. The people of the North refused to sing Fauld's version, since the song was considered disloyal. Faulds stated that Pond paid Emmitt for his words, while he paid Hays nothing for his version. Pond never reprinted Hays's words. He only used Emmitt's words. Unfortunately, the only evidence that history has of this incredible story is Faulds's story. Faulds claimed that in 1894, he lost the only remaining copies of the original version.

Regardless of the controversy over who wrote "Dixie," Hays managed to write three hundred songs over his career and sold more than 20 million copies of his sheet music. He became one of the most prolific songwriters in the United States and was one of the greatest patriotic songwriters of the South. When he died in July 1907, newspapers across the United States paid tribute to him. The *Baltimore News* wrote, "He was one of the most popular song writers this country has ever produced." The *Vicksburg Herald* noted, "His fame rested upon his poetic writings of the old river days, and river men and the old South. There is no one else of his 'quaint individuality' and the mold of such 'picturesque' figures-types of a time that has vanished—is broken. We can no more look for a wearing of his mantle than a return of the old time river boats and their captains. One would be as much out of place in the activities of life in 1907 as the other."[194] William Hays is buried at Cave Hill Cemetery.

Chapter 21

Walter Newman Haldeman and William Birch Haldeman

Both Walter Haldeman and his son, William Haldeman, were leading figures in the newspaper industry, and both were affected by the Civil War. Walter was born in Maysville, Kentucky, on April 27, 1821. He attended the Maysville Academy, later known as the Maysville Seminary. Next to Transylvania University at Lexington, the most famous educational institution in Kentucky during the early 1800s was Maysville Seminary. Among his classmates were William Wadsworth, prominent as a lawyer, forensic orator and member of Congress; Elijah Phister, lawyer, circuit judge and member of Congress; and Union General William Bull Nelson—toward the end of Haldeman's term at school was Ulysses S. Grant. At the age of sixteen, Walter moved with his father to Louisville. He became a clerk in the commission, flour and wholesale grocery house of Rogers & Dunham. The business name was changed to Shreve and Rogers. He also became the proprietor of a horse and dray.[195]

He started his journalism career in 1840 as a clerk in the business office of the *Louisville Daily Journal*, one of the leading Whig newspapers in the West. He left after three years to open a bookstore. He later took over the *Daily Dime*, which became so successful that Haldeman changed the name to the *Louisville Morning Courier*.

On October 30, 1844, he married Elizabeth Metcalf, and on July 27, 1846, she gave birth to William Birch Haldeman. William attended Louisville's public and private schools and later Forest Academy.[196]

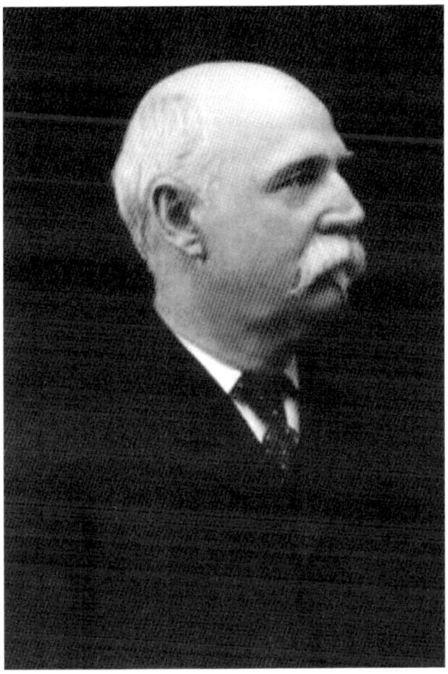

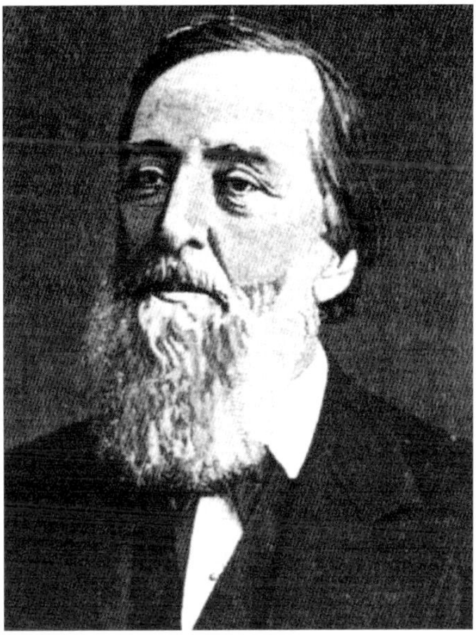

Left: William Haldeman. *Courtesy of the Library of Congress.*

Right: Walter Haldeman. *From Zachary Frederick Smith's* The History of Kentucky: From the Earliest Discovery and Settlement to the Present Date *(Prentice Press, 1895).*

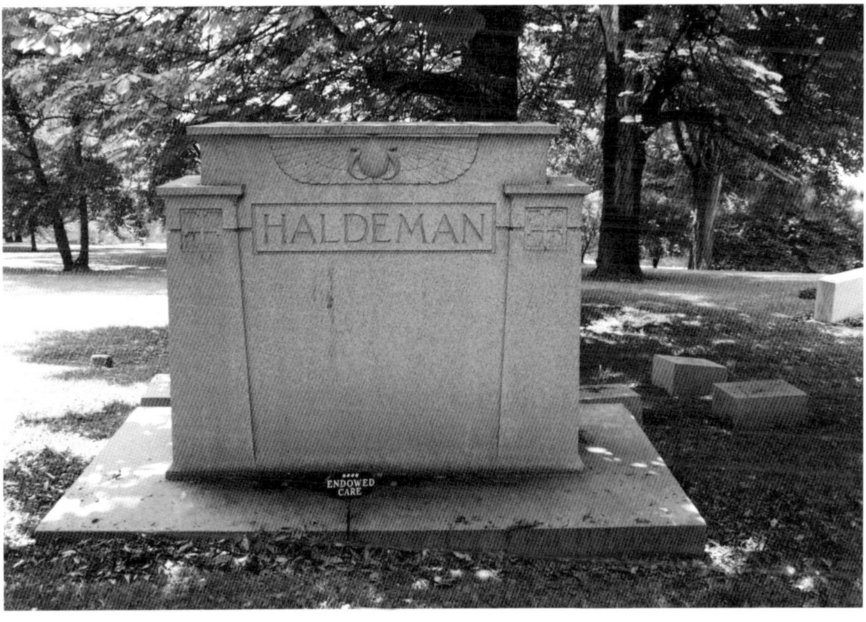

General William Haldeman's gravestone, Cave Hill Cemetery. *Photograph taken by the author.*

As editor of the *Louisville Morning Courier*, Walter Haldeman changed his Whig affiliation radically from nativist to abolitionist and eventually to Southern Democrat, becoming a radical proslavery advocate.

When the Civil War broke out across the country, the *Courier* expressed strong sympathy for the Confederacy. Union authorities seized Haldeman's newspaper and issued a warrant for his arrest. Walter left Kentucky for Tennessee and established the *Courier* in Nashville. Publication ceased when Nashville fell to Union troops in February 1862. Haldeman later fled to Madison, Georgia, where he and his family sat out the war.

When the war began, William left school without permission from his parents, and at the age of fifteen, he joined the Confederacy. In 1862, he served with Confederate General John Hunt Morgan in Tennessee, and in October 1862, during the Confederate invasion of Kentucky, William was entrusted with important dispatches sent by Confederate General John C. Breckinridge, who was in Tullahoma, to Confederate General Braxton Bragg, who was commander of the Army of Tennessee. After the Battle of Perryville on October 8, 1862, the Confederate army left Kentucky, and William followed the retreating army and rejoined Breckinridge's command in Knoxville, Tennessee.[197]

In the winter of 1862–63, William enlisted with Company G, 9th Kentucky Infantry, but in 1864, he was appointed midshipman in the Confederate navy and assigned duty on the CSS *Patrick Henry*, which was lying off the coast of Drury's Bluff on Bermuda Hundred. Prior to the engagement between the commands of Confederate General P.G.T. Beauregard and Union General Benjamin Butler, the crew of the *Patrick Henry* was taken to the fort. During the battle, William had command of one of the guns. Confederate forces repulsed Butler's attack after the fall of Petersburg in August 1864.[198]

William resigned from his position in the navy and rejoined his command in the 9th Kentucky Infantry at Aiken, South Carolina. He remained with the regiment until the surrender at Washington, Georgia, in May 1865.

When the war ended, Walter N. Haldeman returned to Louisville to a hero's welcome. With the help of his friends, he reestablished the *Courier*. In 1868, he bought the *Louisville Journal* and the *Louisville Democrat* and merged the staffs of the *Courier* and *Journal* under the *Journal*'s editor, Henry Watterson. In 1884, Haldeman founded the *Louisville Times*.

After the war, William returned to Louisville and entered the Kentucky Military Institute, graduating in 1869 with a Bachelor of Arts degree. He joined his father's *Courier-Journal* newspaper, but illness forced to him

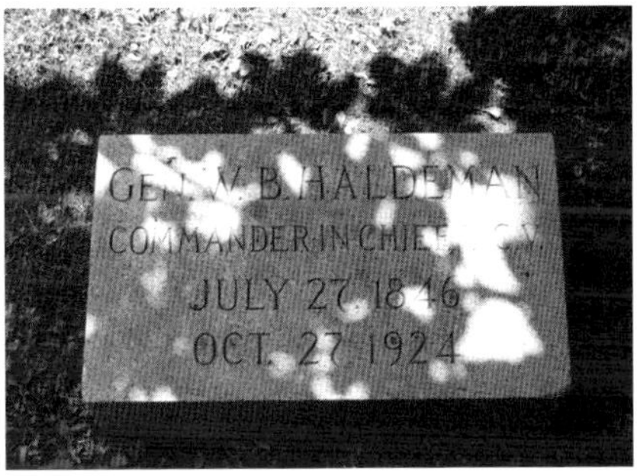

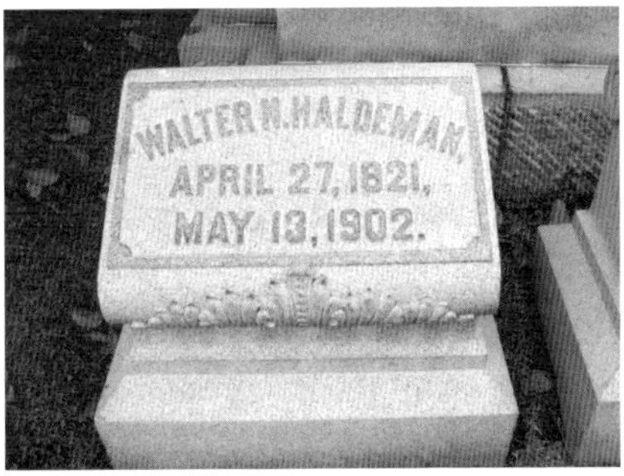

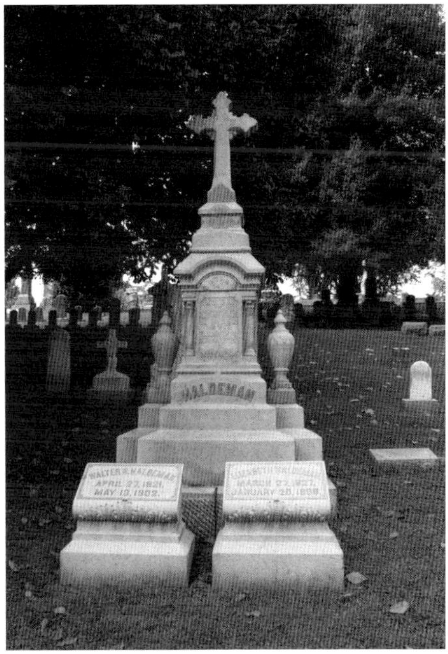

Top, left: General William Haldeman's tombstone, Cave Hill Cemetery. *Photograph taken by the author.*

Bottom, left: Close-up of Walter Haldeman's tombstone, Cave Hill Cemetery. *Photograph taken by the author.*

Right: Walter Haldeman's monument, Cave Hill Cemetery. *Photograph taken by the author.*

move to a better climate in Texas. While in Texas, he studied law and was admitted to the bar.

In 1871, William returned to Louisville and became editor of the *Courier-Journal* and general manager in 1873. In 1885, he was made general manager of the both the *Courier-Journal* and the *Louisville Evening Times*.

On May 13, 1902, Walter N. Haldeman was struck by a streetcar while on his way to the office and died three days later. He left an estate valued at more than $1 million.[199] His son William became editor-in-chief of the *Louisville Times*, and William's brother, Bruce, took over control of the business management of the newspapers. In April 1906, he was elected colonel of the 1st Regiment Infantry, Kentucky National Guard, but resigned in 1909.

In August 1910, General John B. Gordon appointed William commander of the Kentucky Division of the United Confederate Veterans Association with the rank of major general. He died on October 27, 1924.

Notes

Chapter 1

1. Faust, *Historical Times Illustrated Encyclopedia*, 620.
2. Report of Acting Volunteer Lieutenant Edward Morgan, U.S. Navy, late commanding the USS *Signal*, regarding the loss of the vessel during that engagement below Alexandria, Louisiana, May 5, 1864, *Official Records of the Union and Confederate Navies in the War of the Rebellion* (hereafter *ORN*), 1914.
3. Statement of Pilot Perry Wilkes, U.S. Navy, late of the USS *Signal*, regarding of the commanding officer of the USS *Covington* at the time of its loss, May 5, 1864, *ORN*, 1914.
4. Report of Acting Volunteer Lieutenant George Lord, late commanding USS *Covington*, regarding the loss of that vessel during that engagement below Alexandria, Louisiana, May 5, 1864, *ORN*, 1914.
5. Report of Acting Volunteer Lieutenant Edward Morgan, U.S. Navy, late commanding the USS *Signal*, regarding the loss of the vessel during that engagement below Alexandria, Louisiana, May 5, 1864, *ORN*, 1914.
6. *Louisville Courier-Journal*, "Capt. Wilkes Laid to Rest: The Popular Pilot Followed in the Grave by a Host of Friends," March 21, 1889.

Chapter 2

7. *History of the Ohio Falls Cities*, vol. 2.
8. Capps, *Rowan Story*.
9. *History of the Ohio Falls Cities*, vol. 2.
10. Ibid.

11. Ibid.
12. Ibid.
13. Ibid.
14. Ibid.
15. *Official Records of the War of the Rebellion* (hereafter *OR*), January 21–23, 1864—Scout from Rossville toward Dalton, Georgia, and skirmish (22nd), Report of Colonel William P. Boone, 28th Kentucky.
16. Ibid.
17. Ibid.
18. *OR*, November 14, 1864–January 23, 1865—Campaign in North Alabama and Middle Tennessee, No. 53—Report of Lieutenant Colonel J. Rowan Boone, 28th Kentucky Volunteer Infantry, of operations December 15–16, 1864.
19. Ibid.
20. Ibid.
21. Ibid.
22. Ibid.
23. Ibid.
24. Ibid.
25. Ibid.
26. Ibid.
27. Ibid.
28. Ibid.
29. Ibid.
30. Ibid.
31. Ibid.
32. Ibid.
33. Ibid.
34. Ibid.
35. *History of the Ohio Falls Cities*, vol. 2.

Chapter 3

36. Bush, *Civil War Battles of the Western Theater*, 132–34.
37. Ibid.
38. Ibid.
39. Ibid.
40. Ibid.
41. Ibid.
42. Ibid.
43. Ibid.

44. Ibid.
45. Ibid.
46. Ibid.
47. Ibid.
48. Ibid.

Chapter 4

49. Colonel J.T. Macauley, "Loved Character Hears Final Call, Death's Summons Is Answered," *Louisville Times*, November 7, 1915.
50. Ibid.
51. Sifakis, *Who Was Who in the Union*, vol. 1, 247–48.
52. Dyer, *Compendium of the War of the Rebellion*, 11th Indiana Infantry, 1908.
53. Sifakis, *Who Was Who in the Union*, vol. 1, 247–48.
54. Johnson, *History of Kentucky and Kentuckians*, vol. 2, 1,006.
55. Macauley, "Loved Character Hears Final Call."
56. *Louisville Courier-Journal*, "Col. Macauley Laid to Rest Today," November 5, 1925.
57. Kleber, *Encyclopedia of Louisville*, 583.

Chapter 5

58. Under Both Flags: Union Lieutenant Commander Charles W. Flusser, Museum of the Albermarle, 2011, retrieved August 5, 2013; Stewart, *Lion-Hearted Flusser*.
59. Report of William Wells, Acting Master and Executive Officer, U.S. gunboat *Miami*, *Annual Reports of the Navy Department*, 1865; *OR*, series 1, vol. 33 [#60], April 17–20, 1865—Capture of Plymouth, North Carolina, No. 3, Reports of Brigadier General Henry W. Wessells, U.S. Army, commanding subdistrict of the Albermarle.
60. Report of William Wells, *Annual Reports of the Navy Department*; *OR*, series 1, vol. 33 [#60], April 17–20, 1865—Capture of Plymouth, North Carolina.
61. Report of William Wells, *Annual Reports of the Navy Department*; *OR*, series 1, vol. 33 [#60], April 17–20, 1865—Capture of Plymouth, North Carolina.
62. Report of William Wells, *Annual Reports of the Navy Department*; *OR*, series 1, vol. 33 [#60], April 17–20, 1865—Capture of Plymouth, North Carolina.

63. *OR*, series 1, vol. 33 [#60], April 17–20, 1864–Capture of Plymouth, North Carolina, No. 2—Report of Major General John J. Peck, U.S. Army, commanding District of North Carolina.

Chapter 6

64. Bush, *Louisville and the Civil War*, 30.
65. Letter from Thomas Sedgwick to Brigadier General Caldwell, President Military Commission, Washington, D.C., Louisville, Kentucky, May 7, 1864, National Archives.
66. Ibid.
67. Ibid.
68. Ibid.
69. *OR*, series 1, vol. 10, April 6–7, 1862, Battle of Pittsburg Landing or Shiloh, Tennessee, No. 114—Report of Colonel Thomas Sedgwick, 2nd Kentucky Infantry.
70. Ibid.
71. *OR*, series 1, vol. 10, April 6–7, 1862, Battle of Pittsburg Landing or Shiloh, Tennessee—Report of Colonel Sanders Bruce.
72. *OR*, series 1, vol. 52, April 29–June 10, 1862, Advance upon and siege of Corinth and pursuit of Confederate forces to Guntown, Mississippi—Report of Colonel Thomas Sedgwick, 2nd Kentucky Infantry, commanding brigade, of operations April 13–May 30.
73. Ibid.
74. Letter from Thomas Sedgwick to Brigadier General Caldwell, President Military Commission, Washington, D.C., Louisville, Kentucky, May 7, 1864, National Archives.
75. *OR*, series 1, vol. 20, December 26, 1862–January 5, 1863—The Stone's River or Murfreesboro, Tennessee Campaign, No. 127—Report of Colonel Thomas Sedgwick, 2nd Kentucky Infantry, including the skirmish at LaVergne, December 26.
76. Ibid.
77. Ibid.
78. Ibid.
79. *OR*, series 1, vol. 20, December 26, 1862–January 5, 1863—The Stone's River or Murfreesboro, Tennessee Campaign, No. 127—Report of Colonel Thomas Sedgwick, 2nd Kentucky Infantry, including the skirmish at LaVergne, December 26.
80. *OR*, series 1, vol. 30, August 16–September 22, 1863—The Chickamauga Campaign, No 161—Report of Colonel Thomas Sedgwick, 2nd Kentucky Infantry.

81. Ibid.
82. Letter from Major W.H. Sidell, 15th U.S. Infantry to Brigadier General J.B. Fry, postmaster general, Washington, D.C., Louisville, Kentucky, June 2, 1864, National Archives.
83. *New York Times*, "A Mysterious Death: Colonel Thomas D. Sedgewick's Odd Behavior—How He Was Identified," April 27, 1879.

Chapter 7

84. Bryan Bush, "Marcellus Mundy, 23rd Kentucky: A Colonel with a Conscience," *North/South Trader* 30, no. 6 (2004): 50.
85. *Louisville Courier-Journal*, "Death's Hand: Laid Upon Brow of Col. Marc Mundy," February 23, 1901.
86. Ibid.
87. Ibid.
88. Ibid.
89. Ibid.
90. Speed, *Union Regiments in Kentucky*, 513.
91. Letter from Colonel Marc Mundy to President Abraham Lincoln, National Archives.
92. Ibid.
93. *OR*, series 1, vol. 15/1 [S#22], transcript from phonographic notes of the Buell Court of Inquiry, Cincinnati, Ohio, Friday, March 27, 1863.
94. Ibid.
95. Ibid.
96. Ibid.
97. *OR*, series 1, vol. 23/2 [S#35], correspondence, orders and returns relating to operations in Kentucky, Middle and East Tennessee, North Alabama and southwest Virginia, from January 21 to August 10, 1863, Union correspondence, etc. #23.
98. Letter from Colonel Marc Mundy to Secretary of War Edwin Stanton, National Archives.
99. The Abraham Lincoln Papers, Library of Congress, series 1, "General Correspondence," Colonel Marc Mundy to President Abraham Lincoln, March 8, 1864.
100. Ibid., Thursday, July 28, 1864 (colonization).
101. Ibid.
102. *Louisville Courier-Journal*, "Death's Hand"; *Louisville Courier-Journal*, "William Mundy Approaching Death: Bright's Disease Expected to be Immediately Fatal," December 11, 1906

Chapter 8

103. Hafendorfer, *Perryville*, 123.
104. McDonough, *War in Kentucky*, 237.
105. Kentucky Historical Society Marker Database, "On This Spot Brig. Gen. James S. Jackson Fell."
106. Centre College, Kentucky biographies, www.centre.edu; Sifkas, *Who Was Who in the Union*, 210.
107. Bush, *Civil War Battles of the Western Theater*, 38.
108. McDonough, *War in Kentucky*, 253.
109. Bush, *Civil War Battles of the Western Theater*, 40.

Chapter 9

110. *Louisville Courier-Journal*, "To Mother Earth: Funeral of the Late Col. Charles A. Gill, Prosecuting Attorney of the City Court-Action of the Bar," August 23, 1883.
111. Adjutant General's Roll for the State of Kentucky, Charles Gill, 5th Kentucky Cavalry, Company G.
112. *Louisville Courier-Journal*, "To Mother Earth."

Chapter 10

113. *OR*, series 1, vol. 11/1 [s#12], May 5, 1862, Battle of Williamsburg, Virginia, No. 53—Report of Colonel William H. Irwin, 49th Pennsylvania Infantry.
114. *OR*, series 1, vol. 11/2 [S#13], Peninsular Campaign, Seven Days Battles, No. 198—Report of Captain James D. Campbell, 49th Pennsylvania Infantry, of the action at Garrett's Farm and Golding's Farms.
115. *OR*, series 1, vol. 14/1 [s#27], No. 131—Report of Colonel William H. Irwin, 49th Pennsylvania Infantry, commanding 3rd Brigade, of the battles of Crampton's Pass and Antietam.
116. *Cincinnati Enquirer*, "Death of General William Howard Irwin," Special Dispatch to the *Enquirer*, January 18, 1886.
117. Ibid.

Chapter 11

118. *Louisville Courier-Journal*, "Col. Philip Lee: Death of the Brilliant Lawyer and Gallant Soldier," July 13, 1975.

119. Ibid.
120. Thompson, *History of the Orphan Brigade*, 367.
121. Ibid., 368.
122. Ibid.
123. Ibid., 369.
124. *Louisville Courier-Journal*, "Col. Philip Lee."
125. Ibid.
126. Thompson, *History of the Orphan Brigade*, 402.

Chapter 12

127. *Louisville Courier Journal*, "General Harris Passed Away at 11 o'clock Yesterday Morning Was a Remarkable Man in Many Ways," April 10, 1895.
128. Ibid.
129. Ibid.
130. Ibid.
131. Ibid.
132. Ibid.
133. *OR*, series 1, vol. 3 [S#3], September 13–20, 1861—Siege of Lexington, Missouri, No. 4—Report of Brigadier General Thomas A. Harris, Missouri State Guard.
134. *Louisville Courier Journal*, "Gen. Harris Complimented: A Distinguished Soldiers Welcome from His Old Comrades in Arms," October 4, 1891.
135. *Louisville Courier Journal*, "General Harris Passed Away."
136. Ibid.
137. Ibid.

Chapter 13

138. "Joel Mayo Womack," genealogy.com.
139. *Louisville Courier Journal*, "Prisoner's Reunion: Twelve Confederates Who Escaped from Elmira Maj. Womack, of Louisville, and Capt. Berry Benson, of Georgia, Two of Them," April 4, 1900.
140. *Louisville Courier Journal*, "Race History Told by Down's Officer: Major Womack, Track's First Treasurer, Relates Absorbing Stories," September 10, 1910.
141. *Louisville Courier Journal*, "Maj. Womack Will Retain His Position: Compiles Confederate Records," June 18, 1912.

142. *Louisville Courier Journal*, "Secretary of Jacob, When Mayor Is Dead: Joel Womack, 66, Succumbs to Disease Contracted in Costa Rica," June 10, 1921.

Chapter 14

143. Richards, *Mosby's Partisan Rangers*.
144. Broadwater, *Special Forces*, 128–31.
145. Ibid.
146. Ibid.
147. *Louisville Courier Journal*, "Death Claims Judge Richards: Veteran Attorney and Church Supporter Was Widely Known in State," February 21, 1920.
148. Ibid.
149. Levin, *Lawyers and Lawmakers of Kentucky*, 138.

Chapter 15

150. Baird, *David Wendell Yandell*.
151. Ramage, *Rebel Raider*.
152. Ibid.
153. Smith, *Gallant Dead*, 115.
154. Baird, *David Wendell Yandell*.
155. Ibid.

Chapter 16

156. Williams, *My Old Confederate Home*, 13; McNutt, "Life and Times of John Hess Leathers," 2.
157. McNutt, "Life and Times of John Hess Leathers," 2.
158. Ibid. 6.
159. Williams, *My Old Confederate Home*, 13; McNutt, "Life and Times of John Hess Leathers," 2.
160. Williams, *My Old Confederate Home*, 14.
161. Ibid., 15.
162. Ibid., 18–20.
163. Ibid., 20.

Chapter 17

164. *Louisville Courier-Journal*, "Into Clear Waters: Capt. Pink Varble Passes to the Reward He Had Earned," April 3, 1892.
165. *Louisville Courier-Journal*, "Wonderful Feats: The Great Eastern of the Ohio Taken Over the Falls," August 11, 1868.
166. *Louisville Courier-Journal*, "Into Clear Waters."
167. *Louisville Democrat*, November 16, 1861.
168. *Louisville Daily Journal*, January 3–4, 1862.
169. Clark, *Notorious "Bull" Nelson*, 85–87.
170. *Louisville Courier-Journal*, "Into Clear Waters."
171. *Louisville Courier-Journal*, "Smitten at the Wheel: Captain Pink Varble Suffers a Stroke of Apoplexy on the John A. Wood," March 27, 1892.
172. *Louisville Courier-Journal*, "The Falls Pilot Funeral: The Members of Captain Pink Varble Placed in the Tomb," April 5, 1892.

Chapter 18

173. Foster, *Civil War Cards*.
174. *Louisville Courier-Journal*, "Dr. Norvin Green Dying: President of the Western Union Entering the Dark Valley," February 12, 1893.
175. Ibid.
176. Bowen, *History and Battlefields of the Civil War*, 292–93.
177. Ibid.
178. Faust, *Historical Times Illustrated Encyclopedia*, 745.
179. Foster, *Civil War Cards*.
180. *Louisville Courier-Journal*, "Dr. Norvin Green Dying."

Chapter 19

181. *Louisville Courier Journal*, "Called Suddenly: Washington Wyatt, the Well-known Undertaker, Drops Dead at the Breakfast Table," January 8, 1884.
182. Ibid.
183. *Louisville Courier Journal*, "Called Suddenly."
184. Bush, *Louisville and the Civil War*, 95.
185. *Louisville Journal*, October 18, 1861.
186. *Louisville Courier Journal*, "Called Suddenly."
187. Bush, *Louisville and the Civil War*, 110.
188. *Louisville Courier Journal*, "Called Suddenly."

Chapter 20

189. *Louisville Courier-Journal*, "Death Stills Song of Life: End of Will S. Hays, Poet, Songster, Newspaper Man," July 24, 1907.
190. G.E. Johnson, "Way Down South in 'Dixie Land': How the Famous Southern War Song Was Written," *Louisville Courier Journal*, May 29, 1898; *Louisville Courier-Journal*, "Col. Will S. Hays the Real Author of 'Dixie': Death of Dan Emmett Revives Discussion of Authorship of the Famous Songs," July 17, 1904.
191. Ibid.
192. Ibid.
193. Ibid.
194. *Louisville Courier-Journal*, "Newspaper Tributes to Col. Will S. Hays," July 31, 1907.

Chapter 21

195. *Louisville Courier Journal*, "Walter Newman Haldeman," May 14, 1902.
196. Ibid.
197. Johnson, *History of Kentucky and Kentuckians*, vol. 2, 850–52.
198. Ibid.
199. Kleber, *Encyclopedia of Louisville*, 365–66.

Bibliography

The following, in addition to resources at the Library of Congress and the National Archives and Records Administration, were consulted for this work.

Books

Adjutant General's Report for the State of Kentucky. Vol. 1, *1861–1865*. Frankfort: Printed by Authority of the Legislature of Kentucky, 1866.

Adjutant General's Roll for the State of Kentucky. Frankfort, KY: Microfilm, 1935.

Annual Reports of the Navy Department for the Fiscal Year 1864. Washington, D.C.: Government Printing Office, 1865.

Baird, Nancy. *David Wendel Yandell: Physician of Old Louisville*. The Kentucky Bicentennial Bookshelf. Lexington: University Press of Kentucky, 1978.

Bowen, John. *The History and Battlefields of the Civil War*. New York: Wellfleet Press, 1991.

Broadwater, Robert. *Special Forces: The Elite and Distinct Fighting Units of the Union and Confederate Armies.* United Kingdom: Praeger Company, 2014.

Bush, Bryan. *The Civil War Battles of the Western Theater*. Paducah, KY: Turner Publishing Company, 1998, reprint 2000.

———. *Louisville and the Civil War: A History and Guide*. Charleston, SC: The History Press, 2008.

Capps, Randell. *The Rowan Story: From Federal Hill to My Old Kentucky Home*. Bowling Green, KY: Homestead Press Inc., 1976.

Clark, Donald. *The Notorious "Bull" Nelson: Murdered Civil War General*. Carbondale: Southern Illinois University Press, 2011.

Dyer, Frederick. *A Compendium of the War of the Rebellion: Compiled and Arranged from Official Records of the Federal and Confederate Armies, Reports of the Adjutant Generals of the Several States, the Army Registers, and Other Reliable Documents and Sources*. Des Moines, IA: Dyer Publishing Company, 1908.

Faust, Patricia, ed. *Historical Times Illustrated Encyclopedia of the Civil War*. New York: Harper & Row, 1986.

Foster, Stephen. *The Civil War Cards: The People, the Places, the Politics, the Action*. Atlas ed. Durham, CT, 1994.

Hafendorfer, Kenneth. *Perryville: Battle for Kentucky*. Louisville, KY: K.H. Press, 1991.

The History of the Ohio Falls Cities and Their Counties, with Illustrations and Biographical Sketches. Vol. 2. Cleveland, OH: L.A. Williams and Company, 1882.

Johnson, E. Polk. *A History of Kentucky and Kentuckians: The Leaders and Representative Men in Commence, Industry, and Modern Activities*. Vol. 2. Chicago: Lewis Publishing Company, 1912.

Kleber, John. *The Encyclopedia of Louisville*. Lexington: University Press of Kentucky, 2001.

Levin, H. *Lawyers and Lawmakers of Kentucky*. Chicago: Lewis Publishing Company, 1897.

McDonough, James Lee. *War in Kentucky: From Shiloh to Perryville*. Knoxville: University of Tennessee Press, 1994.

McNutt, Kraig. "The Life and Times of John Hess Leathers (1841–1923)." Scribd.com.

Ramage, James. *Rebel Raider: The Life of General John Hunt Morgan*. Lexington: University Press of Kentucky, 1986.

Richards, Adolphus. *Mosby's Partisan Rangers, from Famous Adventures and Prison Escapes of the Civil War*. N.p.: Century Company, 1893.

Sifakis, Stewart. *Who Was Who in the Union*. Vol. 1. New York: Facts on File, 1988.

Smith, Derek. *The Gallant Dead: Union and Confederate Soldiers Killed in the Civil War*. Mechanicsburg, PA: Stackpole Books, 2005.

Speed, Thomas. *Union Regiments of Kentucky*. Louisville, KY: Courier-Journal Publishing Company, 1896.

Stewart, Charles. *Lion-Hearted Flusser: A Naval Hero of the Civil War*. Annapolis, MD: U.S. Naval Institute Press, 1905.

Thompson, Ed Porter. *History of the Orphan Brigade*. Cincinnati, OH: Caxton Publishing House, 1868.

Under Both Flags: Civil War in the Albemarle. "Charles W. Flusser." Museum of the Albermarle, 2011, retrieved on August 5, 2013. http://underbothflags.ncdcr.gov/confederate-decline-characters/charles-w-flusser.html.

U.S. Navy Department. *Official Records of the Union and Confederate Navies in the War of the Rebellion.* Series 1, 27 vols.; series 2, 3 vols. Washington, D.C.: Government Printing Office, 1894–1922.

U.S. War Department. *War of the Rebellion: A Compilation of the Official Records of the Union and Confederate Armies.* Series 1, 53 vols.; series 2, 8 vols.; series 3, 5 vols.; series 4, 4 vols. Washington, D.C.: Government Printing Office, 1886–1901.

Williams, Rusty Williams. *My Old Confederate Home: A Respectable Place for Civil War Veterans.* Lexington: University Press of Kentucky, 2010.

Newspapers

Cincinnati Enquirer.
Louisville Courier-Journal.
Louisville Daily Journal.
Louisville Democrat.
Louisville Times.
New York Times.

Index

About the Author

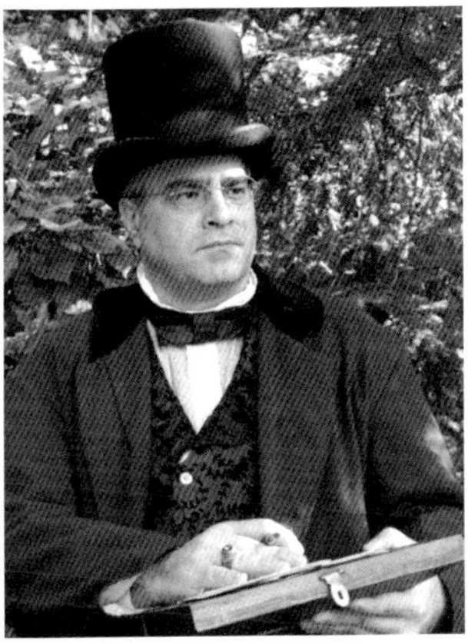

Bryan Bush was born in 1966 in Louisville, Kentucky, and has been a native of that city ever since. He graduated with honors from Murray State University with a degree in history and psychology and received his master's degree from the University of Louisville in 2005. Bryan has always had a passion for history, especially the Civil War. He has been a member of many different Civil War historical preservation societies and roundtables. He has consulted for movie companies and other authors; coordinated with other museums on displays of various museum articles and artifacts; written for magazines, such as *Kentucky Civil War Magazine*, *North/South Trader*, the *Kentucky Civil War Bugle*, the *Kentucky Explorer* and *Back Home in Kentucky*; worked for many different historical sites; and has always fought hard to maintain and preserve Civil War history in the Western Theater. In 1999, Bryan published his first work: *The Civil War Battles of the Western Theater*. Since then, Mr. Bush has had published more than thirteen books on the Civil War, including several titles for The History Press, such as *Louisville and the Civil War: A History and Guide* and *Louisville's Southern Exposition*. Bryan Bush has been a Civil War reenactor for fifteen years, portraying an artillerist. For five years, Bryan was on the board of directors and served as curator for the Old Bardstown Civil War Museum and Village: The Battles of the Western Theater Museum in Bardstown, Kentucky, and is currently a board member for the Louisville Historical League and the official Civil War tour guide for Cave Hill Cemetery.